# The Triumph of Wit

*A Study of Victorian Comic Theory*

by

ROBERT BERNARD MARTIN

CLARENDON PRESS · OXFORD
1974

*Oxford University Press, Ely House, London W.*1

GLASGOW   NEW YORK   TORONTO   MELBOURNE   WELLINGTON
CAPE TOWN   IBADAN   NAIROBI   DAR ES SALAAM   LUSAKA   ADDIS ABABA
DELHI   BOMBAY   CALCUTTA   MADRAS   KARACHI   LAHORE   DACCA
KUALA LUMPUR   SINGAPORE   HONG KONG   TOKYO

ISBN 0 19 812057 5

© *Oxford University Press 1974*

*Printed in Great Britain by*
*Butler & Tanner Ltd*
*Frome and London*

*To the memory of*

E. L. H.

# PREFACE

IT must be immediately apparent to anyone reading a late Victorian comic work (for example, one by Meredith or Butler or Shaw) that it is vastly different from most works written forty or fifty years earlier. The subject-matter is different, of course, but what really sets it apart is the tang of wit and intellect that seems so different from the flavour of Hood or Praed or most of Dickens, Thackeray, and Trollope. Many of the late Victorians actually seem to have a good deal more in common with such eighteenth-century writers as Sterne or Swift or Fielding than they do with their immediate predecessors. This book is an attempt to document the change of comic theory in the Victorian period, from a belief in amiable, sentimental humour to an acceptance of intellect as the basis of comedy.

This is not the place in which to discuss whether criticism moulds artistic creation or merely records it; suffice it to say that I believe the process to be one of mutual influence. I do not intend this book as a study of the comic practice of the great Victorian writers, however influential, only as a record of the background of theory against which they wrote. This is not to scant their achievement or even their influence, merely to indicate that the focus is on the critics' changing ideas about comedy. There is much to be learned about the subject from the practice of such writers as Dickens or Trollope, but that investigation lies outside the scope of this study.

Some years ago I began thinking about a book on the comic practice of a number of Victorian writers. Naturally, one of the prime documents I read frequently was Meredith's *Essay on Comedy*, the best-known theoretical work on the subject in the century. Slowly I realized what I should have recognized long before, that I did not totally understand that apparently easy piece of theory. The trouble was not in the diction, opaque though that is, but in the assumptions that Meredith made, confident that his contemporaries would understand the unstated problems with which he was dealing. To remedy my own ignorance, I began reading widely in other Victorian criticism. It soon became apparent that the theory of comedy had changed as radically as the practice. I became increasingly interested in the change, and from that interest the present study sprang.

The first half of the book deals with the inherited beliefs of the Victorians about comedy; with the conflicting theories of superiority and incongruity as the sources of comedy; with the opposition of humour and wit; with contrast and comparison as opposing explanations of wit; and with the conflicting claims of the Imagination and Fancy. Throughout the Victorian era there is a gradual shift towards the acceptance of incongruity and wit as the essence of comedy. In the second half of the book I examine some of the major Victorian theorists of comedy, including Sydney Smith, Leigh Hunt, Thackeray, George Eliot, Leslie Stephen, George Meredith, and that curious group, the phrenologists. As a general pattern, it is fair to say that the later the criticism, the further it is apt to have moved away from an acceptance of sentimental humour.

The writers I have concentrated on are those critics who were interested in comedy as literature, which means that many famous writers are not treated here. For example, there is no mention of Darwin and Spencer, who were chiefly interested in the physical aspects of laughter, and little of James Sully, who was primarily concerned with the psychology of laughter. Bagehot and Macaulay, though they were prompted to write about comedy, were not basically interested in speculation about its nature. And perhaps the greatest of Victorian literary critics, Arnold, seems to have been profoundly uninterested in comedy. As Northrop Frye has said, Arnold's touchstones derive from tragedy and the epic, and 'his demotion of Chaucer and Burns to Class Two' was apparently prompted by a belief that 'comedy and satire should be kept in their proper place, like the moral standards and the social classes which they symbolize'.* One has the feeling that those contemporaries of Arnold's who insisted on his wit did so with an earnest insistence that may have reassured themselves but only reveals to others that the characteristic in question never existed.

It has been necessary to curtail the discussion of the forbears

* *Anatomy of Criticism* (Princeton, 1957), p. 22.

of the critics here presented, so that there has been little or no space in which to consider the theories of Plato, Aristotle, Congreve, Barrow, Hazlitt, Hogarth, or Fielding, to mention only a few of the names that come to mind at once when thinking of comedy. Instead, I have concentrated on those critics who most directly influenced Victorian thinking on the subject.

Somewhat arbitrarily, I have stopped the history at 1877, the year Meredith lectured on the idea of comedy. This is not intended to suggest that he was the culmination of thought towards which comic theory had been struggling during the century; rather, it seems to me that his consideration of the subject coincided with a period of wholesale revision of theory. After his *Essay* there was plenty of theoretical writing, but the change from a belief in the supremacy of humour had already been accomplished. There was an increasing tendency for comic theory to pass from the literary critics to the psychologists and philosophers. The contributions of such men as Bergson and Freud is another story.

One of the difficulties of writing about this subject is the inevitable repetition of phraseology that is inexact at best. As must already be apparent, by 'comedy' I mean the manifestation of the comic spirit in all forms of literature, not the dramatic alone, although that is the primary signification of the word; there is, unfortunately, no convenient term to indicate the broader meaning. Similarly, 'laughable', 'risible', and 'ludicrous' are used interchangeably, although all of them are awkward, and 'ludicrous' has the usual meaning of absurdity in modern speech. To invent new terminology, however, makes reading as cumbersome as does the usage of older, inexact terms, so I have settled for familiarity rather than neologism.

In any book written with conviction or love, it seems to me a transparent deception to pretend that the author is marmoreally dispassionate. I have predispositions and beliefs about comedy, and I may as well confess them. My own enthusiasm is for wit, the comedy of language and idea and intellect, as must be obvious to the reader of what follows. Not because I despise amiable or sentimental humour, but because that seems to me to provide a more constricting way of regarding the world than does wit. If I read comedy aright, wit may easily include a good bit of sentiment (and even sentimentality) in its purview, but the reverse is not true. This confession is not intended for purposes of conversion but simply to save the reader the trouble of trying to locate my own prejudices, in order to discount them in reading the book.*

Since the days of Jeremy Collier critics have often given implicit assent to his views by confusing the proscenium arch with the pulpit. If I am correct in my views, comedy stops when the preaching begins. Early Victorian critics seem to me to be totally mistaken in thinking that intellectual comedy is immoral; it is neither moral nor immoral in itself, although morality may well be its subject, and even its result. Surely, if Collier was wrong in deploring the immorality of comedy, it is equally fallacious to assert its morality. This is not to say that one learns nothing from comedy, only that the educative qualities inherent in it are not immediate. Illumination, not moralizing or didacticism, is the purpose of art.

Briefly, comedy seems to me to be like all other forms of artistic activity: a way of giving meaning and shape to inchoate experience. At its best, like all art, it heads directly into the centre of life and sheds light on what it finds there. It is not escapist; it is engagist (if there were such a word). To fail to take it seriously is to discount a vast and important area of human artistic experience. But to take it earnestly and lugubriously is to miss the point of this branch of art. Critics who demand formulated instruction from comedy are like those religionists who speak of procreation as the only purpose of sexual activity; both apparently lose sight of the fun involved. (Indeed, in both cases one may sometimes wonder if it is not the means that justifies the end.)

This book will be a disappointment to those friends who have said plaintively that studies of comedy are never funny, and that they hope I shall rectify the matter. It is an attitude that seems to me to indicate a fairly low opinion of comedy and a belief that it is hardly worth taking seriously (at least, it would indicate something of the sort if they were someone else's

---

* Anyone who is interested in my views on the subject will find them in more complete form in 'Notes Toward a Comic Fiction', in *The Theory of the Novel: New Essays*, ed. John Halperin (Oxford University Press, New York, 1974). In the present volume I have tried to keep them at a minimum.

friends, not mine). Actually, there is no more reason to expect that a history of comic theory will be hilarious than that an account of pulmonary diseases in the boot-and-shoe trade should be. I do not expect to be purged by a history of tragedy, made vertiginous by a book on mountaineering, or to have my feet set tapping maniacally by a catalogue of the compositions of Cherubini. I should have no objection whatsoever to being able to make my readers collapse in uncontrollable laughter, but that is unfortunately not the purpose of this book, even if I had such talents, so I can only hope that I am not guilty of dismal earnestness, although that is no more than I should expect of any book, whatever its subject or author.

It is impossible to name all those to whom I am grateful for help, but it would be ingratitude of the crassest kind to neglect thanking Princeton University, the American Council of Learned Societies, and the John Simon Guggenheim Memorial Foundation for giving me time and support in various stages of the project; the Bodleian Library, the British Museum, and the Princeton University Library, in which places most of the research was done, for their assistance; Professor Walter E. Houghton and the Wellesley Index to Victorian Periodicals for the attributions of anonymous articles. Above all, I am indebted to the late Edward L. Hubler, wisest of colleagues and wittiest of friends, for the countless delightful and instructive hours in which we discussed comedy and comic theory. Had he survived to give me his peppery advice on the writing of this book, I am sure it would have been immeasurably improved.

*Wootton, Woodstock, Oxon.*, 1972

# CONTENTS

## CHAPTER I

# The Dangers of Laughter

THE average reader probably has two clear but contradictory pictures of the Victorian age. One is of a stiffly buttoned gentleman in top hat and impeccable broadcloth, with mutton-chop whiskers complementing, but not hiding, the earnest face that regards the world around in a direct, unsubtle, complacent, and above all humourless, expression. The other is of an expansive figure with flat hat, buttons straining over a Falstaffian belly (certainly not that of a gentleman), and a red face creased in a broad grin never hidden except by the pot of ale in his hand. Unlike they certainly are, but there is some justification for believing them both to be representative of important Victorian attitudes. Agelasts and hypergelasts, George Meredith conveniently labelled them in his quirky fashion: the non-laughers and the excessive laughers.

The Victorians were much concerned with the propriety of laughter: whether it was suitable for philosophers, for Christians, even for ladies and gentlemen (they were, after all, immediate descendants of Lord Chesterfield, who claimed that he had not been observed to laugh since attaining to his sober maturity). By extension the validity of comedy and of the risible in literature was brought into question. Probably our hypothetical average reader remembers Arnold's Scholar-Gipsy fleeing from the clatter of the ale-house on the Berkshire downs, and the grave Tyrian trader in the same poem flying the laughter and racket from the intrusive young sailors on the merry Grecian coaster. Possibly there is more reason to think of those agelastic young men as typically Victorian (or, at least, mid-Victorian) than there is to call to mind as an emblem of the age a Dickensian figure of mirth in a coaching inn, looking like the quintessential Toby-jug.

It was not merely a question of whether comedy and laughter were proper; if they were acceptable, in what form were they to be couched? From this question sprang the whole series of choices with which this book is concerned. Should comedy be amiable, an affair of the sympathetic heart, even sentimental; or ought it be a product of the intellect, appealing back to the source from which it sprang? Should the risibilities be touched by humour or by wit? And what was the attitude in the writer and in reader and audience that caused the creation and appreciation of comedy: was it a sense of superiority to someone else, or was it an awareness of the incongruities between aspiration and achievement, between ideal and actual? And how did the mind work in comic perception: by distinguishing between unlike things or by seeing likeness in apparently dissimilar objects and ideas? And should comedy be the result of the workings of the Imagination or of the Fancy? Not easy questions, certainly, and not surprising that so much should have been written to try to answer them. Yet for all the diversity in the questions, what they all boiled down to was asking whether comedy had a serious function in the world, or whether it was to be dismissed as a frivolous and perhaps dangerous form of amusement.

Though we probably have no difficulty in imagining emblematic figures for the agelast and the hypergelast, it is less easy to conjure up a vision of a witty mid-Victorian face looking humanely malign, as Meredith postulated the countenance of comedy should; the face fits easily enough beneath the wigs of the Restoration and the eighteenth century, and it sits comfortably above the velvet lapels of the Decadents, but it is not at ease beneath a top hat. When Meredith was looking for examples of the best comedy, according to his lights, he found that 'notwithstanding the wealth of our literature in the Comic element, it would not occupy us long to run over the English list'. His contemporaries were politely ignored.

Some years ago Howard Mumford Jones wrote that 'the nineteenth century has actually given more first-rate humorists to English literature than any other century in the long roll of English letters'. His proposition is primarily devoted to showing that it is probably our century, not the preceding one, that is lacking a sense of humour, and one can assent to the statement, but it is less easy to agree that 'the wit of the century which invented *Punch* is perhaps its most enviable possession'.[1] The writers he cites in support of his statement chiefly offer examples of humour not wit. Neither of these terms is easy to define, to be sure (it is part of the purpose of this book to show how their meaning changed during the course of the nineteenth century), but if one accepts the classification of comedy of character and comedy of intellect and idea as indicating the distinction between humour and wit, the basic point is clear. It is more than chronology that separates *Pickwick* from *The Way of All Flesh*; 'Miss Kilmansegg and Her Precious Leg' from *The Egoist*; or *The Yellowplush Correspondence* from *Man and Superman*. Between such extremes is a whole world of difference about the nature and function of comedy, and it is that changing world with which we shall be concerned.

As a general pattern, it might be said that comedy during the reign of Queen Victoria changed from sentimental comedy to the comedy of wit and paradox. Unfortunately, the world does not change neatly and completely, as an historian might prefer it to do; nor does literature follow the diagrams that would be most convenient to indicate its course: Jane Austen, for instance, and Peacock preceded Dickens. All the same, the pattern has some validity.

What are undoubtedly the two best-known Victorian works on comedy come from the pens of men known more widely as novelists than as critics: Thackeray and Meredith. In 1851 Thackeray's lectures on *The English Humourists of the Eighteenth Century* looked backward to the great writers whom he judged more by character than by either comic practice or literary talent. In 1877 Meredith lectured *On the Idea of Comedy and the Uses of the Comic Spirit*. The very titles of the lectures indicate the shift of emphasis from character to theory, which was a clear parallel to the change of interest in comedy from personality to idea, from humour to wit.

For all their differences, Thackeray and Meredith had in common a singular lack of reference to comic writing in the middle of Victoria's reign. Thackeray looked back to another century for his models, Meredith across the Channel. In spite of Thackeray's fulsome tribute to Dickens at the end of 'Charity and Humour', he must have realized that his own theories about comedy were already a bit dated. A quarter of a century later Meredith was painfully aware that though the weight of

B

critical opinion was swinging around to his view of the matter, the man in the street still had little idea of comedy as connected, even distantly, with intellect. It is in part because Thackeray was somewhat at odds with the change in critical thought, Meredith alienated from popular taste, that neither piece of criticism can really stand alone as a statement about Victorian comic theory, let alone the practice of so diverse an age.

To pick out two partially unsatisfactory pieces of critical writing as the most famous of their time is not to suggest that they took their fame by default and that there was a paucity of comic theory at the time. Quite the contrary, as anyone can testify wearily who has slogged through the thousands of repetitive pages written on the subject at the time. Unfortunately, most of the theory was produced by pedestrian writers, even anonymous hacks, and it is frequently to them that we must turn to find out what the Victorians thought about what was usually called 'the ludicrous'. Over and over they copied the catalogue of facetiousness from Isaac Barrow, the similes from Butler, the strictures against laughter of Chesterfield, the definitions of Hobbes and Locke, usually adding nothing original of their own. None the less, the cumulative evidence becomes very clear as to the changing taste among Victoria's subjects.

Reliance upon the writings of second-raters for an explanation of what the great writers were up to is obviously a dangerous process. It is too reminiscent of, say, those studies of Shakespeare explaining him as a typical Elizabethan: elucidation of the miraculous by the mundane, measurement of the extraordinary by the pedestrian. But the process can have its uses, too. Writers like Dickens, Thackeray, Trollope, and Meredith were keenly aware of what both reviewers and readers thought. Hack theorists usually reflected what the reading public demanded—or would in the immediate future. Middle-class taste, tyrannous though it is, does occasionally illuminate literary practice.

It demands considerable self-possession to believe that laughter and comedy are valid ways of viewing the world, even to accept them as wholesome human activities, for comedy is in part dependent upon the triumphant revelation of a discrepancy between the ideal and the actual, and it is never safe to make that kind of revelation unless one is so confident of the fundamental unity of the world as to be able to laugh at the apparent chinks in its solidity. Notoriously, Puritans have been haters of laughter, and the great burgeoning middle class in the nineteenth century was the Puritan body of the population, as well as the core of the reading public. Like other Puritans they were exigent about behaviour and surface decorum, while they were afraid of the churning emotions just beneath that surface. When one realizes that chaotic emotion and decorum will always be in conflict, then superimposes upon that knowledge the awareness that even conflict is part of a unified world, it finally becomes safe to laugh at comedy, either in the world around us or in literature. That realization, that safety, was precisely what the Victorian middle class lacked. It was dangerous to laugh because laughter revealed the fundamental dislocation of both the individual and society.

The problem was not specifically Victorian; what the crowd's reaction was at the first phallic procession is not recorded, but we can probably assume safely that some few were shocked at the revelation of an aspect of human nature normally hidden decently. From the beginnings of Christianity there has been some doubt about the propriety of risibility. Saint Paul, whose associations with the comic seem otherwise remote, warned the Ephesians that it behoved saints never to mention fornication, covetousness, 'neither filthiness, nor foolish talking, nor jesting, which are not convenient'. Whatever convenience may have to do the matter, he was clearly equating jesting with witlessness and sin.

It is perhaps salutary to remember that in our century one of the greatest barriers to the election of Adlai Stevenson as President of the United States was his wit; it is still difficult for many people to believe in seriousness of purpose without heaviness of manner. Self-doubt, worry, fretfulness seem to them more adequate demonstrations of concern than the confidence and assurance that allow a man to be playful with ideas, and lack of ease is thought to be a better indication of trustworthiness than confidence. Tragedy will always be taken more seriously than comedy, and melodrama will be more popular than either.

Any one who has taught literature to university under-graduates will know that they frequently respond to comic novels or poems but discount them for their very urbanity. Their response to Jane Austen may be more immediate than to lumpish earnestness in, say, Lawrence, but it will seem to them somehow more decorous to consider the latter seriously, simply because he never arouses a laugh. In our own Puritan age, no one is more Puritan than the liberated young, no one more frightened of levity. When almost anything goes morally, our horror seems reserved for comedy. Let one plod laboriously through the sludge of existence and there is no question of the value of the sheer plod; once laugh at existence, however, and the hands raised in horror wave like a field of corn.

All the same, however trivial one may think comedy, it is never acceptable to be thought lacking in a sense of humour; this almost universal contradiction of our own day seems to have made its appearance during the nineteenth century. 'A fashion has sprung up of late years of regarding the sense of humour as one of the cardinal virtues,' Leslie Stephen wrote in 1876. Another writer, in the *Saturday Review*, had come to the same conclusion a few years earlier:

If you tell a man that he has no poetical faculty, no talent for mathe-matics, no genius for oratory, or for natural science, or for meta-physics, he will very likely agree with you; he may even admit, though that is less common, that his logic is not remarkable for clearness or precision, and he will very often consent with surprising readiness to be pronounced deficient in any of the Christian virtues. But we have never known anybody who would frankly confess that he was without a sense of humour.

What is so commonly claimed, however, is seldom allowed to one's neighbours. The French, we are told, have no 'real sense of humour', that of the Germans is 'of the humblest kind', the Scots (as Sydney Smith had said) require a surgical operation to get a joke into their understanding, 'and, in short, if we except a few Englishmen, Irishmen, and Americans, the whole world is in a state of utter darkness'. Some English writers would not have allowed such a state of light to the Irish and Americans.

The fact is, said Stephen, that 'the most dangerous of all

figures of speech is the ironical'. Half of those who proclaim their sense of humour with pride 'think that you are laughing at virtue, and the other half have a puzzled impression that you are laughing at themselves'.[2]

Much Victorian theory about comedy hovered uneasily between the extremes of proclaiming its virtues and worrying that it was inappropriate for serious persons. In 1862 it was actually proposed that laughter should be taken as the subject of one of the Bridgewater Treatises, which were concerned with elucidating the nature of God: 'For there are aspects of highest wisdom in many of the forms of wit, and Divine life may and does shine through much that only creates laughter.' Yet, even in exalting so highly the function of laughter, the writer was careful to indicate its built-in dangers. 'Far be it from us to inculcate or to commend the habit of regarding everything from its comic or a comic side [sic]. This can be neither Christian, manly, nor healthy.'[3]

In 1869 W. H. Lyttleton attempted cautiously to rehabilitate the good name of laughter and make it an honest woman in Victorian literature (the fact that he felt called upon to do so is probably a better indication of the low repute into which it had fallen than his actual résumé of popular opinion on the subject). But he also felt a pressing need to be cautious about advancing its claims, and to admit that it was constantly open to abuse. Almost every argument he propounds is countered by some such statement as, 'Now, I am far indeed from denying that there is such a thing as "excessive laughter", or that it may be, and often is, a source of serious mischief.' Like most of the other writers who acknowledged its danger, he was somewhat vague about what the location was of the line that divided excessive laughter from that which was permissible. 'It is not all men who can be trusted with much freedom of jesting; it is only good men, and all of us only so far as we are good, with whom "joy is its own security", and the free "abundance of the heart" is sure not to sin against good taste and good feeling, or even against some of the most sacred laws of God.' One wonders whether Lyttelton knew of any one besides himself who fulfilled such stringent qualifications.

Laughter was apt to usurp the place of more serious modes of thought, according to Lyttelton. What could be more provoking than those who dissipated their energies in levity, 'pulling out that stop in the midst of serious and profitable discussion, whether at public or private meetings, and so let off, not superfluous, but most useful steam, which otherwise might have done invaluable work'? In fine it was a matter of discipline, for Lyttelton thought that hearty laughter '*need* not be in the least against *good manners*', nor was it essentially 'something coarse'. To believe in its coarseness was 'a poor, a thin, a meagre, and an unchristian morality'.[4]

Samuel Bailey thought that though 'their best specimens have a ground-work of good sense and substantial thought', wit and humour 'may be sometimes out of place, and sometimes carried to excess'.[5]

Even more outspoken was the writer in the *Westminster Review* who worried over the fact that 'the sense of the ridiculous, like all the other faculties of our minds, has its own appropriate sphere of action, the bounds of which, however, it continually oversteps'. It had been summed up succinctly by Goethe, who was said to have claimed that 'One cannot have a sense of humour unless one be without conscience or responsibility'.[6] The spectre of immoderate laughter was one to which even the supporters of the risible and ludicrous had to give a ritual nod.

In part, the dread of too much laughter was a simple fear of being guilty of social impropriety, of the sort that one assumes Chesterfield felt. In part, however, it sprang from a desire to shield the innocent. When family fireside reading was an established custom, it was necessary to avoid novels or poetry that would give offence to the wives and daughters of the household. Stephen cautioned Thomas Hardy always to 'Remember the country parson's daughters'.[7] Probably the danger to the young ladies' faith meant little to either Stephen or Hardy; the injunction was intended to keep the writer from impropriety that would make his books unacceptable in such a circle. Delicacy of this sort in feminine readers was probably not widespread before the 1850s. By 1871 it could be stated seriously that 'women are too good to be humorists. They are too pure and saintlike and enthusiastic to understand masculine cynicism, and they hate to be told that any cause to which they have given their affections has after all a tinge of absurdity.'

Comic perception was 'not quite compatible with the possession of the highest Christian virtues'.

A humorist may be a thoroughly excellent and amiable person; but he is hardly likely to be a saint. We cannot imagine the loftiest spiritual nature having the full appreciation of a joke. We have known some very good men who liked puns and small witticisms; but we have always found them rather shocked even by the innocent varieties of humour. The humorist, in fact, has just that tendency to look at the seamy side of things, and that delight in bringing high emotions to the test of some vulgar or grotesque association, from which the man of saintly nature characteristically shrinks.

A very different opinion was that of the writer who said that 'a woman has no natural grace more bewitching than a sweet laugh'.[8] The difference was perhaps that between writer and audience; women might read or hear what they were not permitted to write or speak.

For obvious reasons, humour throughout the history of the world has frequently concerned itself with either the sexual or the scatological; however careful one might be, the Victorians knew, laughter tended towards the obscene, and even when it did not, it was associated by long tradition with obscenity. Such a belief one writer called 'a dreary creed', for the 'opposition of the class of enemies to humorous writing, is founded on the belief, that vulgarity and wit are synonymous, and that mirth is incompatible with "gentility" '.[9]

The *Westminster Review* said that it was difficult to exaggerate the temptations to overstep the limits of good taste facing the writer 'who is constantly expected to write wittily'. But the best of writers could resist the temptation, for in all the writings of Thomas Hood, 'there is not a line which one would hesitate to read aloud in the family circle'.[10]

What was probably even more deep-seated than the fear that laughter might involve the innocent in obscene matter was the belief that unchecked comedy had as its disguised goal the putting of holy matters into disrepute, that religion itself might be flouted. 'Laughter is from its nature more easily allied to contempt and egotism than to affection and devotedness,' the *Westminster* noted in 1847. 'But we must consider laughter also as a philosophy, a mental support and consolation against the ills of life. . . . There is a certain seriousness in keeping with the realities of life, and the laughing, and all other philosophies that blind us to these, only lead us to destruction.' Some years later another article in the same periodical said that when the sense of the ludicrous intrudes upon grounds 'the most solemn and most sacred; it then becomes an influence as injurious as, in its proper field of exertion, it is beneficial'.[11]

Proof that religion should not be treated with levity (and, indeed, that serious Christians should beware of lightness in any case) was frequently given by citing the fact that the Bible records the occasion on which Jesus wept, but there is nothing to indicate that He laughed. Leigh Hunt was writing in deadly earnest when he defended laughter against this kind of attack by his own invocation of Biblical authority: 'A name, to which we would not be supposed capable of lightly alluding . . . did not hesitate to let itself be found among the sitters at a marriage feast, where wine was drunk, and cheerfulness, nay mirth, is not easily to be supposed to have been wanting.'*

Religion might have seemed to be forever linked with sobriety, but there were already signs of a recognition that it need not suffer from a comic approach. The writer who pro-posed that laughter might be made the subject of a Bridgewater Treatise said that no one can fail to believe that even good men laugh (and his attitude was certainly not the result of slackening religious beliefs, whatever might have been the cause of the loosening elsewhere of prohibitions against the mirthful treat-

* 'On the Combination of Grave and Gay', in *Leigh Hunt's Literary Criticism*, ed. L. H. and C. W. Houtchens (New York, 1956), p. 565. Samuel Butler at a later date was satirizing the kind of reasoning displayed by both sides of the controversy when he wrote in *The Way of All Flesh* of Ernest's attempts to give up smoking: 'We can conceive of St. Paul or even our Lord Himself as drinking a cup of tea, but we cannot imagine either of them as smoking a cigarette or a churchwarden. Ernest could not deny this, and admitted that Paul would almost certainly have condemned tobacco in good round terms if he had known of its existence. Was it not then taking rather a mean advantage of the Apostle to stand on his not having actually forbidden it? On the other hand, it was possible that God knew Paul would have forbidden smoking, and had purposely arranged the discovery of tobacco for a period at which Paul should be no longer living. This might seem rather hard on Paul, considering all he had done for Christianity, but it would be made up to him in other ways' (chap. 50).

ment of sacred matters). 'That highest, holiest, men, great reformers and martyrs, have obtained their irresistible influence over their fellow-men by their skill in wielding the weapons of humour—rousing even to very mirthful views of things—who can doubt?' In 1866 Leslie Stephen defended the American habit of mixing profane and sacred by saying that the modern English usage of treating the Bible respectfully by separating it carefully from common life 'is a piece of refinement incomprehensible to minds which have not yet been made so sensitive by education. We would rather not decide which practice shows most belief, though it is plain which shows most reverence.'[12]

The whole question of whether it was proper to be comic about sacred subjects was a reformulation by the Victorians of a controversy that had exercised the previous century. Probably it is fair to say that there is no such thing as a totally new theory about comedy, and that this state of affairs has existed for two or more centuries; certainly, every aspect of what the Victorians were worrying about in this matter had been anticipated in a relatively obscure controversy provoked initially by the third Earl of Shaftesbury at the beginning of the eighteenth century.

The subject of the whole somewhat tedious fracas is usually referred to as 'ridicule as the test of truth', although the phrase was not Shaftesbury's. Dozens of answers were written (largely to questions that he had not propounded), and for at least a century and a half the phrase was capable of inciting speculation, not to say wrath. Like many furious but essentially trivial theological disputes, it provoked response because of its implicit assumptions not because of the overt grounds upon which the argument was reared. Today it is important only emblematically, for what lay behind the whole controversy was the question of whether comedy and laughter were only diversions, and disreputable ones at that, or whether they were to be treated as modes of intellectual investigation, whether they were ways of thinking or mere scornful ticklings: in short, whether they might serve as instruments in the austere search for truth—or even Truth.

'I have often wondered', wrote Shaftesbury in 'A Letter Concerning Enthusiasm', in 1709, 'to see men of sense so mightily alarmed at the approach of anything like ridicule on certain subjects; as if they mistrusted their own judgment. For what ridicule can lie against reason?'[13] The question seems both clear and innocuous. He is apparently defending the impregnability of reason against hostile risibility, advancing the unexceptionable doctrine that truth can never be finally downed by erroneous laughter. Or, to turn the proposition around, that man can afford to play with ideas that are secure; probably only men who are certain of their wives laugh very heartily at stories of cuckolds.

Shaftesbury had been prompted in his 'Letter' by the desire to show that the best way of dealing with bigotry and false enthusiasm was to ventilate it with the fresh wind of laughter; in the event he was nudged into writing by the excessive—and to him repugnant—behaviour of certain French religious refugees who had antagonized their English hosts. Rather than repress the Frenchmen, Shaftesbury was suggesting, one should make them the object of laughter.

But the world is full of unlaughing cuckolds, and religion—and religiosity—has some followers who are afraid, probably subconsciously, that it will not hold up to the rough-and-tumble of humour. What is sacred, they say, should be exempt from laughter. Almost immediately Shaftesbury was attacked for going too far, for not knowing where to draw the line. In response he attempted to clarify his position in *An Essay on the Freedom of Wit and Humour.*

Truth, 'tis supposed, may bear all lights; and one of those principal lights, or natural mediums, by which things are to be viewed, in order to a thorough recognition, is ridicule itself, or that manner of proof by which we discern whatever is liable to just raillery in any subject.[14]

Not only is ridicule a criterion of truth, but it becomes a defensible, even necessary, mode of investigating the truth of a belief or proposition. What cannot bear such searching light cannot be true. The subject, however, is somewhat complicated by the notoriously loose diction of Shaftesbury's writing. By 'ridicule' he seems here to mean a form of derision, but at other times the word appears to be equivalent to any kind of wit, humour, even good temper. If he is using ridicule in its primarily derisive connotation, he is agreeing with Hobbes and his theory of superiority as the cause of laughter, and it is easy to see why the assumption and application of such a theory to religion irritated so many of his contemporaries.

Even easier to understand is the hostile reaction to three apparently mischievous propositions that he set forth in his *Miscellaneous Reflections*:

1st. That wit and humour are corroborative of religion, and pro-motive of true faith.
2nd. That they are used as proper means of this kind by the holy founders of religion.
3rd. That notwithstanding the dark complexion and sour humours of some religious teachers, we may be justly said to have in the main a witty and good-humoured religion.[15]

It has been said that Shaftesbury was providing a philo-sophical basis for the satire of the eighteenth century.[16] What seems more important, no matter what meaning he was giving to ridicule, is that he was stating the case for not confining wit, comedy, and laughter to the trivialities of life for their province, and that they are a perfectly valid form of inquiry into those most important areas of morality, philosophy, and religion. Not only could patent error be subjected to comic investigation, but even those topics previously prohibited from such investiga-tion could be looked at by the light, whether warm or cold, of comedy. It is a statement of considerable importance to the history of comic theory.

But we must not assume that Shaftesbury consciously in-tended all this. Chiefly he was concerned, in a perfectly tradi-tional, Hobbesian way, with the comic as a mode of exposure of immorality and imposture. 'For nothing is ridiculous except what is deformed; nor is anything proof against raillery except what is handsome and just.'[17] However, in stating his views he probably suggested more than he knew. Indeed, the very ambiguity (presumably unintentional) of what he wrote was probably responsible for the almost incredible number of essays written in response; almost no two of them were in agreement about what they were refuting, and to the modern reader there is no surprise about their confusion.

One historian has said that 'Furious as the controversy may have been in the eighteenth century, it did not extend itself into the nineteenth . . .'[18] This is not strictly true, although most of what there was to say on the original subject had been repeated before the nineteenth century; over and over, to tell the truth. 'Ridicule as the test of truth' really lost all sense of the original controversy and was used as a handy phrase to indicate almost any questioning of whatever one held most sacred. No longer was it necessary, or even desirable, to refer to Shaftesbury or to define his position; the mere mention of ridicule was sufficient to evoke all the impropriety of comedy.

Some indication that the heat of the controversy had not died with the light is the perturbation with which Carlyle could write of it as late as 1829. Ridicule 'is directly opposed to Thought, to Knowledge, properly so called; its nourishment and essence is Denial, which hovers only on the surface, while Knowledge dwells far below'. Of that doctrine which he said was 'vulgarly imputed to Shaftesbury', he could only demand indignantly to know 'who gave laughers a patent to be always just, and always omniscient?'[19]

The danger that the eighteenth century had seen in ridicule was still apparent to Alexander Bain, reviewing Leigh Hunt anonymously in the *Westminster* in 1847. There is probably some truth, he thought, in what cannot be dethroned by derision or by alliance with degrading ideas, but 'the opinions that defy ridicule in one age often sink under it in another'.[20]

The *Eclectic Review* provided a somewhat surprising echo of Shaftesbury's belief in the comic as a way of looking at the truth about religion. Its defence of laughter as a bulwark of Christianity called ridicule 'the literary detective' and '*the logical power of laughter*, for logic can avail itself of the force of ridicule to destroy a folly . . .'[21]

By 1876 Leslie Stephen could still refer to the controversy with no apparent sense that it was a dead one, and, like practically everyone else who had entered the lists, he took the occasion to write about his own beliefs, rather than what Shaftesbury had said. What Shaftesbury and the *Eclectic Review* had thought of as a support to Christian truth became in Stephen's hands a great destructive force to help agnosticism rout the old superstitions. 'The use of such modes of controversy necessarily jars upon reverent minds,' he noted gleefully. 'When a phantom dogma persists in haunting the living world, a laugh will cause it to vanish more rapidly than the keenest logical slashing. . . . The pedant tries to maintain his superiority, no longer resting on physical force, by an attitude of excessive solemnity. The obvious retort is to laugh at him.'[22]

It is instructive to see how often Shaftesbury's ideas were turned into something quite different by other men. Not surprisingly, his contemporaries who attacked him misrepresented what he had said in order to demolish his position. What is perhaps less predictable is that a century and a half after Shaftesbury innocently began it, historians of the controversy were still grinding their own axes. James Sully in 1877 represented Shaftesbury as saying that any idea which *could* be laughed at was false or illogical. The point of view is very different from that of Leslie Stephen, but it shares his belief in laughter as hostile and destructive to false doctrine. Between the poles of that belief and Shaftesbury's own belief that what was true or logical could be laughed at without invalidating it, stretches a wide spectrum of attitudes towards comedy. The subject is made more complex when one realizes that both Stephen and Sully on other occasions were to adopt attitudes more like Shaftesbury's own.[23]

The dates of the works by Stephen and Sully are interesting, for their authors may well have contributed to George Meredith's consideration of comedy. On 1 February 1877 he lectured nervously on comedy at the London Institution; the first publication of the lecture was in the *New Quarterly Magazine* of April that year. It is, to say the least, not improbable that he would have discussed the subject with his friend Stephen and read his remarks about it. Sully's essay was published anonymously in the *Cornhill*, of which Stephen was editor. Shaftesbury is not mentioned in Meredith's *Essay*, but the controversy underlies much of the work.

It is perhaps fair to give the last word on Shaftesbury to that splendidly confused man, Mr. Brooke of *Middlemarch*. When he attempts to make a political speech in standing for Parliament, he is pelted with eggs and mocked by the crowd. 'Buffoonery, tricks, ridicule the test of truth—all that is very well,' he says unhappily (chap. 51). It is difficult to penetrate his disappointed diction, but one can assume that he gives less than total assent to the doctrine; 'we never heard of any one who, voluntarily, became a laughing-stock for the purpose of testifying the sincerity of his opinions', as a writer in the *Westminster* remarked on another occasion.[24] George Eliot set her novel in the first half of the nineteenth century, but in 1872 she could write the phrase in clear confidence that her readers would still understand the reference.

## CHAPTER II

# The Claims of the Intellect

I N the 1860s and 1870s other changes were overtaking the consideration of laughter and comedy, with a gradual shift from belief in superiority as the source of the risible, to an acceptance of its basis being in various forms of the incongruous; parallel with this ran the growing acceptance of wit as a valid form of language and way of looking at the world, and a change from the pre-eminence of amiable humour to that of comedy of the intellect.

Classical and Renaissance critics had often located the essence of comedy in the essentially satirical, but it was Thomas Hobbes whose definition of scorn as the central factor in laughter was most frequently quoted by the Victorians for the neatness of his formulation:

*Sudden glory*, is the passion which maketh those *grimaces* called LAUGHTER; and is caused either by some sudden act of their own, that pleaseth them; or by the apprehension of some deformed thing in another, by comparison whereof they suddenly applaud themselves. And it is incident most to them, that are conscious of the fewest abilities in themselves; who are forced to keep themselves in their own favour, by observing the imperfections of other men. And therefore much laughter at the defects of others, is a sign of pusillanimity. For of great minds, one of the proper works is, to help and free others from scorn; and compare themselves only with the most able.*

In *Human Nature* Hobbes calls laughter the '*sudden glory*

* *Leviathan* in *English Works of Thomas Hobbes*, ed. Sir William Molesworth (1839, reprinted 1962), III, 46. The passage, like many from the primary documents concerning comedy, was often reprinted without much knowledge of the original, and occasionally the words 'sudden glory' led unwary theorists into believing that Hobbes subscribed to a theory of amiable humour. See, for example, Frank Penthorne, who wrote that 'Thomas Hobbes of Salisbury said many a wise thing in his time, but never anything wiser or more beautiful than this: "Laughter is a sudden glory" '. ('Vis Comica', *Belgravia*, XXIV [September 1874], 331).

arising from some sudden *conception* of some *eminency* in ourselves, by *comparison* with the *infirmity* of others, or with our own
formerly'. The admission of superiority that men feel to 'the
follies of themselves past' takes part of the sting of hostility out
of the definition, but the truth is that Hobbes thought of
laughter chiefly as derisive and vainglorious about the deficiencies of others: 'the passion of laughter proceedeth from a *sudden
conception* of some *ability* in himself that laugheth. Also men
laugh at the *infirmities* of others, by comparison wherewith their
own abilities are set off and illustrated.'

Victorian recognition of the hostility at the root of laughter
was a fair reading of Hobbes; laughter could be the reaction
of little minds only, except in those rare cases where he admitted
that it might proceed from '*absurdities* and infirmities *abstracted*
from persons'. The 'distortion of the countenance which we call
laughter' is always a product of joy, but it is usually the joy of
triumph over another. Hobbes was also stern about excessive
'*mobility* in the spirits', which 'is another defect of the mind,
which men call *levity*'. The virtue opposite to levity 'is *gravity*, or
steadiness'.[1]

Like many other philosophers who are widely quoted,
Hobbes was useful less for providing new ideas than for giving
validation and respectability to beliefs that the Victorians
already held. The frequency with which he was quoted tells us
more about what the Victorians wanted to believe than it does
about their reading of Hobbes.*

If laughter was really only the outer rictus indicating an
inner scorn and pusillanimity, it became clear that it was the
duty of the decent, charitable man to avoid laughing, on moral
as well as social grounds. There was as yet no Freud to point
out that laughter was a relatively harmless way of giving vent
to one's aggressions, and it is doubtful that such a suggestion
would have been entertained, in any case.

---

* The general view of superiority is still far from dead; perhaps the most
thoroughgoing exposition of it in this century is by Anthony M. Ludovici,
in *The Secret of Laughter* (1932), where 'show teeth' is used as a synonym for
'laugh', comedy is chastised for shirking the solution of thorny problems by
laughing at them, and humour is held responsible for the downfall of king-
doms, the breakup of marriages, the dominance of women, and most of the
other ills to which man is heir.

There remained, however, another possible way of explaining the basis of laughter, and it might initially seem to offer a way of combining decent motivation with the undeniable pleasures of comedy and the risible. It has been a commonplace in most studies of comedy that there are two general types of theory: that which we have been examining, the Hobbesian theory of superiority, and a second type that ascribes comedy and laughter to the perception of incongruities. There are, as we shall see, certain fundamental likenesses between the two types of theory, and each of them is capable of division into more exact definitions, but most comic theory can be subsumed under these two general headings.

The distinctive mark of the theory of incongruity is that it substitutes an intellectual perception for a moral one: 'instead of setting behind our enjoyment of the ludicrous an emotion, or a change in our moral attitude, namely, a sense of our own superiority or of something else's degradation, it sets a purely intellectual attitude, a modification of thought-activity', according to James Sully. Both parts of the incongruous, whether persons, ideas, or actions, may be perceived objectively, without direct reference to ourselves. Thus, the discrepancy between protestation and actual accomplishment may strike us as ludicrous without directly involving a comparison with ourselves. Or the incongruity may relate directly to ourselves; whatever makes us laugh at ourselves, for instance, must be personal, but it obviously need not be evidence of a feeling of superiority.

Laughter is accounted for in the theory of incongruity, according to Sully, as a result of 'a peculiar effect on our intellectual mechanism, such as the nullification of a process of expectation or of an expectant tendency'.

As has been suggested, the theory of superiority ultimately made laughter condescending and aggressive; the theory of incongruity, by substituting intellectual perception for the awareness of moral superiority, seemed to do away with the unpleasantness of what was clearly an enjoyable activity, and which had once seemed harmless as well.

In Sully's view, the explanation of the ludicrous in terms of the incongruous is 'characteristically German', and 'Kant may be taken as the first great representative of this theory'. But the fact is that this theory of the comic is at least as old as Aristotle, and one might notice that a far more influential proponent of it in nineteenth-century England than any German was Coleridge, although his ideas admittedly derived in part from German thinkers.[2]

Kant's own contribution is largely confined to a few sentences. 'In everything that is to excite a lively convulsive laugh there must be something absurd (in which the Understanding, therefore, can find no satisfaction),' he wrote. '*Laughter is an affection arising from the sudden transformation of a strained expectation into nothing.*' His primary interest was in the physical manifestation of the perception of comedy rather than its cause: the ludicrous is 'a mere play of representations bringing about an equilibrium of the vital powers in the body', since 'with all our thoughts is harmonically combined a movement in the organs of the body'.[3] However, behind these brief comments lies a theory of incongruity between anticipation and result.

Schopenhauer carried the idea of disparity further, into the realm of paradox. Apparently he thought that laughter is caused by 'incongruity between a concept and the real objects that had been thought through it in some relation'. Elsewhere he wrote that the ludicrous depends upon the contrast 'between representations of perception and abstract representations'. Paradox may be either the final revelation of true congruity between apparently incongruous objects, or it may be, less typically, the ultimate revelation of actual incongruity between apparently like objects. The paradoxical is 'the subsumption of an object under a concept that is in other respects heterogeneous to it'. All laughter, Schopenhauer explains, is therefore 'occasioned by a paradoxical, and hence unexpected, subsumption, it matters not whether this is expressed in words or in deeds'. With his usual arrogance he dismisses all other attempts at theorizing: 'This in brief is the correct explanation of the ludicrous.'

Like most of what he wrote, Schopenhauer's explanation of the comic is not exactly limpid, but he seems to have believed that wit lies beyond the merely ludicrous, as paradox lies beyond the apparently congruous or apparently incongruous. When 'two or more apparently very different real objects, representations of perception or intuition' are 'arbitrarily identified . . . through the unity of a concept embracing both; this species of the ludicrous is called *wit*.'[4]

Essentially, what Schopenhauer is suggesting is that the paradox is the display of the falsity of a syllogism because the minor premise is unexpected and only valid sophistically, and that it is the exposure of the falsity in thinking which lies at the heart of laughter. Although his beliefs are couched in language concerned with the intellect, it is obvious that exposure of false reasoning (particularly when it is the reasoning of another) comes very close to a kind of superiority, removed from Hobbes's formulation more by language than by essence.

Probably most English aestheticians of the first three quarters of the nineteenth century would have known little of Schopenhauer, and he is not mentioned by name in any of the criticism of the period that I have seen. What is more important than the question of direct influence is the fact that the general drift of theory was in the direction of intellectual incongruity as the basis of the ludicrous, paralleling his thinking, even if not derivative from his writing.

What we can be certain about is that Coleridge knew the works of Kant, and that either in imitation of the other philosopher, or on his own, he had rejected superiority as the basis of comic perception. 'To resolve laughter into an expression of contempt is contrary to fact, and laughable enough.' Aristotle's definition of the laughable 'is as good as can be:—surprise at perceiving anything out of its usual place, when the unusualness is not accompanied by a sense of serious danger'. It seemed natural to Coleridge that the highest form of the ludicrous came about when the finite was put into incongruous contiguity to the infinite. 'In the highest humour, at least, there is always a reference to, and a connection with, some general power not finite, in the form of some finite ridiculously disproportionate in our feelings to that of which it is, nevertheless, the representative, or by which it is to be displayed.' The syntax is tortured, the meaning clear. 'Humorous writers . . . delight, after much preparation, to end in nothing, or in a direct contradiction.' It is a restatement in his own terms of Kant's 'sudden transformation of a strained expectation into nothing'.

Comedy and wit may be used, according to Coleridge, for mere entertainment or as a means of speculation, 'though where the object, consciously entertained, is truth, and not amusement, we commonly give it some higher name'. Whatever the name, Coleridge is obviously extending the function of wit and the comic to areas totally inaccessible to laughter dependent upon a contemptible sense of personal superiority.[5]

Gradually there began to take place a blurring of the distinction between the theory of incongruity, as applied to all the risible, and the definition of wit, which previously had been treated as only one part of the ludicrous. In the major piece of comic criticism of the 1840s Leigh Hunt took notice of the change in the meaning of wit, which had previously still retained some of its older associations of intelligence and understanding having no necessary connection with laughter: 'in the popular and prevailing sense of the term (an ascendancy which it has usurped, by the help of fashion, over that of the Intellectual Faculty, or *Perception* itself), Wit may be defined to be *the Arbitrary Juxtaposition of Dissimilar Ideas, for some lively purpose of Assimilation or Contrast, generally of both.*'

Hunt also attempted a resolution of the theories of superiority and incongruity by suggesting a singular meaning of 'triumph' that left no one defeated. When mirth is pure, the only superiority we feel is to 'the pleasant defiance' that is offered to our wit and comprehension. In such a case 'we triumph, not insolently but congenially; not to anyone's disadvantage, but simply to our own joy and reassurance.'[6]

An unfriendly critic in *Fraser's* commented upon the remarkable similarity of Hunt's definition of wit to that of Coleridge, and said that the latter had described it 'shorter and better, as resulting from the detection of the difference in similar and the identity in dissimilar things'. (It must surely have been the only occasion on which Coleridge was congratulated on his brevity.) The reviewer did not, however, mention Hunt's usage of wit as comprehending all of intellectual comedy; it was a merging of meaning already too well established to call for comment.[7]

'It is admitted on all hands', said the *Westminster* review of Hunt's book, by Alexander Bain, 'that incongruity is the cause of laughter. We are not aware of any case that yields the ludicrous where there is not some inequality or incompatibility in the degrees of reverence or respect that an object inspires.

A creature incapable of worship is incapable of laughter.'[8] Such an admission was far from universal, whatever Bain might say, but the statement does indicate a trend towards the popular acceptance of the theory of incongruity, an acceptance that did not become anything like complete for another thirty years. 'As the intellect ripens . . . we learn to laugh as we learn to reason,' wrote another critic at about the same time, showing the unquestioning way in which laughter and reason were beginning to be associated in some minds.[9]

There were, however, several reasons why it was difficult for many Victorians to accept a theory of comedy that depended upon incongruity or the intellect. It did seem initially to avoid the appearance of moral condescension or malice implicit in the theory of superiority, but, as we have seen in the case of Schopenhauer, some of the formulations of the theory of incongruity appeared to suggest an intellectual arrogance scarcely pleasanter than one concerned with morality.

So nervous were some critics about advancing a theory fundamentally divorced from moral emotions that they tried to make incongruity itself a form of moral consideration. This view was put forth most forcefully by H. D. Traill near the end of the century:

The incongruous is the unfit, the unsuitable, the discordant, the imperfect; it covers generically half a score of more specific adjectives which are names not of honour but of reproach, and all the associations of which, *save in the one case in which humour emerges from them*, are associations not of pleasure but of pain. The incongruous is the unsymmetrical, the disorderly, in one word the *wrong*. And yet man, whose one natural motive impulse upwards, after the satisfaction of his bodily needs, is the instinct of pursuit after, and delight for their own sakes in, order, symmetry, fitness, in one word the *right*, is capable of taking the keenest pleasure in the contemplation of their opposites. Why is this?[10]

Coleridge had attempted to separate the intellectual and the moral by saying that 'the true ludicrous is its own end. . . . The true comic is the blossom of the nettle.'[11] But this was to enunciate still another reason for believing that comedy was inappropriate for serious-minded persons. At least, the theory of superiority had posited a real use for comedy and laughter: the identification of the immoral, the stupid, or the contemptible, with the suggestion that its identification would lead eventually to its eradication. Such comedy might be unpleasant in tone, but it finally promoted morality, prudence, and sanity. To say that the ludicrous was its own end was to rob it of all utility, and there were few things the Victorians feared more than the useless. Utilitarianism was far more than a mere philosophical label; it was the fabric of middle-class thought. When Matthew Arnold asked for sweetness and light, and when Newman tried to define a liberal education, they were combating the deeply engrained prejudices of a civilization that judged ideas by their immediate practicality. The shock that ran through England at the hard, gem-like brilliance of the Decadents at the end of the century was less at positive immorality than at a conception of life that denied utility. It has even been suggested that part of the reason sexual activity was so carefully hidden in Victorian society was that it was a notorious waster of energy, with little to show for it, except in a Malthusian sense.

Although Carlyle believed, in general, that laughter should be amiable and as therapeutic as cold baths and keeping the bowels open, he preferred even superior laughter to that of the intellect, as postulated by Kant and Coleridge. 'One right peal of concrete laughter at some convicted flesh-and-blood absurdity,' he said of Coleridge at Highgate, '. . . how strange it would have been in that Kantean haze-world, and how infinitely cheering amid its vacant air-castles and dim-melting ghosts and shadows!'[12]

We can easily see, then, the cleft stick in which the Victorians were struggling. If comedy were backed by morality, and valuable for its educational potential, then it finally appealed to scorn, arrogance, and contempt. The alternative seemed equally bad. If the major force of comedy were an intellectual one in which scorn was discarded and laughter became its own end, then it was hard to see that it had any utility. In neither case was it something that could be acceptable to those who were both kindly and practical; few Victorians would have admitted lacking either of those qualities, any more than they would have admitted to having no sense of humour.

## CHAPTER III

# Wit and Humour

A s Victorian critics seldom tired of saying, it is not easy to distinguish between wit and humour (not that the difficulty seemed to prevent their trying). Totally unlike in meaning originally, the two terms had edged towards each other in usage in the seventeenth and eighteenth centuries and by the nineteenth were so overlapping as not often to be distinguished except by philosophers, psychologists, or critics. Today the distinction between them is so blurred that it would probably seem pedantic to most persons to regard them as separate aspects of comedy and the ludicrous.

It is not my purpose to give a history of the change of meaning of the two words except as that change concerned the Victorians, but it may be worthwhile considering briefly what their inheritance was in the matter.*

Over the centuries humour had changed its significance from moisture (and hence the four chief fluids of the body) through the mental qualities, moods, and personalities associated with the four fluids, to a general reference to quaintness, vagaries, and eccentricity. By the eighteenth century the meaning in common usage referred to speech, writing, action, or thought that excites amusement and laughter by its oddity. This in turn led to the modern usage of the word to refer to almost anything associated with laughter.

The change from the Restoration to Victorian times is summarized succinctly by Stuart Tave:

In Restoration theory of comedy . . . it was a commonplace that the function of comedy is to copy the foolish and knavish originals

---

* The change in the meaning of humour from the Old English period to the eighteenth century is amply dealt with by Louis Cazamian in *The Development of English Humor* (Durham, N.C., 1952). Its subsequent history in the eighteenth and early nineteenth centuries is traced by Stuart Tave in his admirable study, *The Amiable Humorist* (Chicago, 1960), which shows how the supposed coldness of wit slowly yielded to the warmth of a sentimental humour. To this latter excellent book I am much indebted.

of the age and to expose, ridicule, satirize them. By the middle of the nineteenth century, it was a commonplace that the best comic works present amiable originals, often models of good nature, whose little peculiarities are not satirically instructive, but objects of delight and love.[1]

Wit originally indicated the seat of consciousness or thought, then progressively became associated with intellect, reason, and understanding, then with the whole of the mental faculties. Through a natural linkage it changed to meaning celerity, acumen, talent, and general facility of those faculties. By the seventeenth century the term was increasingly applied to thought, speech, or writing that surprised and delighted by its neatness and surprise, usually occasioning laughter.

By the opening of the nineteenth century wit and humour were the two processes most often thought to produce laughter (although there was genuine doubt as to whether the best humour actually did so), and both were subsumed under the terms of comedy (which included but was not usually confined to the stage), the risible, and—most frequent of all—the ludicrous. The usual distinction between comedy and wit was that used later by the *Oxford English Dictionary*, where humour is 'distinguished from *wit* as being less purely intellectual, and as having a sympathetic quality in virtue of which it often becomes allied to pathos'. The matter seemed settled, and so it appeared until three quarters of the century had passed.

The eighteenth century had been quite as perplexed as their descendants about the scorn, degradation, and condescension implicit in the superiority theory of comedy. Briefly, their solution to the problem had been to concentrate on personal aspects of humour, then to exaggerate the sympathy that one must feel in order to have total perception of individuality or eccentricity, so that the object of humour provoked laughter *with* it, not *at* it, finally to make sympathy and love the really distinguishing aspects of humour, as laughter dropped away from it. (Indeed, it almost seemed as if the provocation of laughter was proof that writing was *not* humorous.) The standard examples advanced were those of Sterne's Uncle Toby and (improbable as it may seem to the twentieth century) his story of Le Fever; Don Quixote; and Falstaff in his more amiable aspects.

Carlyle may be taken as a typical representative of the early Victorian attitudes to humour and wit, and for him the great antithesis of the two kinds of comedy was exemplified by Jean Paul Richter and Voltaire: the loving humorist and the cold mocker. Of Richter's humour he wrote that

Like all his other qualities, it is vast, rude, irregular; often perhaps overstrained and extravagant; yet, fundamentally, it is genuine Humour, the Humour of Cervantes and Sterne; the product not of Contempt, but of Love, not of superficial distortion of natural forms, but of deep though playful sympathy with all forms of Nature.*

As it was for Carlyle and the Romantics, humour became the more praiseworthy for the later Victorians because of its vastness, rudeness, and irregularity, since those qualities indicated that it was not the product of the 'superficial distortion' of literary art; it was 'natural', with all the overtones of that approbatory word indicating a harmony with the Divine Forces rather than with the mere intellectual powers of man. Richter's 'Humour, with all its wildness, is of the gravest and kindliest, a genuine Humour; "consistent with utmost earnestness, or rather, inconsistent with the want of it".' The greatest of humorists was not subject to the decorum of the neo-classical school, but neither was he without order. 'A Titan in his sport as in his earnestness, he oversteps all bound, and riots without law or measure. . . . Yet the anarchy is not without its purpose. . . . Love, in fact, is the atmosphere he breathes in, the medium through which he looks.' His humour gives form to 'Inanimate Nature itself . . . with which he communes in unutterable sympathies'.

'The essence of humour is sensibility,' Carlyle announced firmly; 'warm, tender fellow-feeling with all forms of existence.' Schiller had said that the last perfection of our faculties came about when their activity had become sport, without losing either their sureness or their earnestness. True humour, for

* Quotation from 'Jean Paul Friedrich Richter', *Critical and Miscellaneous Essays*, II, 146. There it is quoted from 'one of Richter's English critics', with whose views Carlyle saw 'little reason to disagree'. Such agreement is less than startling, since Carlyle himself was that critic ('Jean Paul Friedrich Richter', in *German Romance*, II, 122–3). To confuse the matter further, Carlyle wrote three essays bearing the same title.

Carlyle, was 'this *sport* of sensibility; wholesome and perfect therefore; as it were, the playful teasing fondness of a mother to her child'. The quality of his metaphor itself is indicative of the sentimentality lying behind his conception of humour.

All the Romantic and Victorian distrust of the intellect is implicit in Carlyle's praise of 'true humour', which 'springs not more from the head than from the heart; it is not contempt, its essence is love; it issues not in laughter, but in still smiles, which lie far deeper'. The intellect, the head, contempt, laughter: all are lumped together (however unconsciously on Carlyle's part) in opposition to loving smiles proceeding from the heart. For a moment he has forgotten the Titanic laughter of Richter as he reverts to the preconceptions of his age.

More than Carlyle's habitual overstatement is at work when he compares, albeit inversely, the functions of the humorous and the sublime. Humour 'is a sort of inverse sublimity; exalting, as it were, into our affections what is below us, while sublimity draws down into our affections what is above us'. For the Romantics and early Victorians the conceptions of humour and the sublime shared ruggedness, grandeur, and, finally, the transcendental lineaments of the divine. The beliefs and enthusiasms of any period may be gauged by the terms that it blunts metaphorically from their original meanings into that of routine praise. As 'natural' became a term of approbation without real reference to Nature, so 'miraculous', in a more devout age, came to mean simply 'first-class', with little remaining sense of Christian miracle. To Carlyle the equation of humour with the sublime was a form of compliment in which the precise original eighteenth-century connotations of the sublime were probably forgotten, although their aura remained, indicating the vague, almost religious respect in which he held humour.

A different statement of the same point was made in Carlyle's essay on Schiller, in which he said that humour 'is properly the exponent of low things; that which first renders them poetical to the mind. The man of Humour sees common life, even mean life, under the new light of sportfulness and love; whatever has existence has a charm for him.'[2] What, one is tempted to ask, has happened to laughter?

Such a notion of humour as that held by Carlyle and his contemporaries is not only a proceeding against wit and the intellect; it is really a denial of the function of comedy and the ludicrous, for to make them acceptable, one has kept the names and removed the content. The truth about the controversy over the nature of humour is that its concern was actually about whether humour—in the sense of risibility that the seventeenth century and the later nineteenth century knew—really had any acceptable function at all. And the answer was that it had not for the late eighteenth and early nineteenth centuries.

Since it is the contention of this book that the last quarter of the nineteenth century began once more to recognize the importance of wit and comedy as valid modes of perception, it would be convenient to assert that from the time of Carlyle forward, there was a progressive awareness of the limitations of sentimental humour. It was not so. All during the period there were occasional nods in the direction of the intellect as an integral part of comedy, but more often critics pressed the claims of humour as a warm suffusion of the loving, charitable emotions, in striking contrast to the arid sneers of wit.

Charles Dickens was perhaps not an unprejudiced critic, but his views on humour reflected widespread attitudes about it as much as they helped create those attitudes. Eccentricities well understood, he thought, yield sympathy not laughter. In the preface to the reprinted *Pickwick Papers* he admitted that his most popular comic figure, Mr. Pickwick, undergoes a decided change in character during the course of the novel, and that he becomes better and more sensible.

I do not think this change will appear forced or unnatural to my readers, if they will reflect that in real life the peculiarities and oddities of a man who has anything whimsical about him, generally impress us first, and that it is not until we are better acquainted with him that we usually begin to look below these superficial traits, and to know the better part of him.[3]

What the theories of both superiority and the incongruous postulated was sufficient distance from the object of comedy to perceive how it was out of joint. What sentimental comedy, like that of Dickens, advocated was the eradication of that distance and an identification between perceiver and perceived.

Richter was often quoted as an example of what humour ought to be. De Quincey thought that his characteristic distinction among Germans 'is the two-headed power which he possesses over the pathetic and the humorous'. De Quincey then continues to make evident the unspoken assumption that wit and the intellect are immoral, or at best amoral. Wit is intellectual, he says, but humour has 'an influx of the *moral nature*'.[4]

Leigh Hunt characteristically recognized the virtues of both humour and wit, although he distinguished between their subject-matters. Humour 'derives its name from the prevailing quality of *moisture* in the bodily temperament; and is *a tendency of the mind to run in particular directions of thought or feeling more amusing than accountable*; . . . It deals in incongruities of character and circumstance, as Wit does in those of arbitrary ideas.'[5]

The moist origins were elaborated on by the American critic Edwin P. Whipple. 'Humour originally meant moisture—a signification it metaphorically retains, for it is the very juice of the mind, oozing from the brain, and enriching and fertilising wherever it falls.' While wit laughs at others, 'humour laughs *with* them'. As Whipple warmed to his subject, he almost inevitably suggested that humour is too high for laughter, since it 'has the earnestness of affection'. Like Carlyle he said that it lifts 'what is seemingly low into our charity and love', and to do that 'implies a sure conception of the beautiful, the majestic, and the true, by whose light it surveys and shapes their opposites'.

As if all this were not enough with which to credit humour, Whipple said that since wit is negative, analytical, and destructive, and humour creative, it is only the masters of humour who can create great characters in fiction, since they operate by way of sympathetic feeling. 'Wit cannot create character. . . . It cannot create even a purely witty character, such as Thersites, Benedict, or Beatrice.'[6] If the claim seems excessive, it is so only if one does not accept the equation of humour and love, since it was a truism that no writer could create a believable character without loving him.

Humour 'may be defined as the flavour of character', said Mortimer Collins in 1870. Further, it 'has a permanence of character, and will bear reiterated study', unlike the flash of wit that can never achieve its effect twice. Unlike wit once more, it is natural, for the 'humorous man is born so; no one was ever born an epigrammatist'.[7]

Like those who live in almost any age of considerable sentimentality, the Victorians believed that the highest form of sympathy and love consisted of shared tears. Easily, almost imperceptibly, the sympathy that was the mark of humour became identified with pathos. 'The greatest humourists have often been also the most serious seers, and men of most earnest heart,' wrote Gerald Massey. 'Hence their humour passes into pathos at will.' And the pathetic becomes the measure of the humorous, since 'the deepest humour and pathos will often be found in twin relationship'. Tears and pathos, however, might ultimately be provocative of happiness at the deepest level, and they were not to be confused with actual sadness, for the influence of both wit and humour can be benign if it 'makes us forget sad thoughts and cankering cares'.[8]

Amiability, sympathy, naturalness, pathos: these had become the identifying characteristics of humour, and how widely they were accepted as such by the Victorians can be verified in nine-tenths of the critics. Humour is 'never unallied with sympathy'; it 'lies nearer to nature' than wit; it is 'the flavour of character'; it takes 'pleasure in extracting laughter from tears, or *vice versa*'; the 'highest mark of the humorous character—perfection in itself' comes when 'the ridiculous and pathetic' are 'blended into one'; laughter is near akin to 'genial, beneficent tears'; a humorous writer 'is good-natured... he bears no malice'.[9]

It would, of course, be nonsense to suggest that there was a particular moment after which humour ceased to mean all these things, or even that the term suddenly ceased to be used. All the same it is true that the unquestioning acceptance of its meaning seems to have changed somewhere before 1877, which is when Meredith gave his lecture on the Comic Spirit. (It is instructive to see how seldom he referred directly to humour.) Meredith's attitude may have influenced others, but it is more probable that he reflected what was becoming an increasingly widespread attitude towards comedy. The eighteenth century had redefined humour to suit its changing conception of the comic, but a hundred years of usage of that redefinition had so firmly entrenched the newer meaning that at the end of the nineteenth century the term gradually dropped out of critical language, rather than being given still another definition. In common usage, of course, it always retained the sense of the ludicrous that had been current in the late seventeenth century and that has persisted until our own day; there is often a conservative bottom of good sense in the language of the vulgar that eludes critics.

Wit, Edwin Whipple wrote in 1850, was 'originally a general name for all the intellectual powers', then its usage was contracted 'to express merely the resemblance between ideas; and lastly, to note that resemblance when it occasioned ludicrous surprise'. Always, however, there remained some remnant of intellect as distinguished from emotion. 'It marries ideas, lying wide apart, by a sudden jerk of the understanding.'[10]

The formulations of the meaning of wit most often quoted by the Victorians, and to which they were most indebted in their thinking, were those of Hobbes and Locke. Both condemned wit in part, and both set it in direct opposition to the better functions of judgement.

Natural wit, according to Hobbes in *Leviathan*, consists principally 'in two things; *celerity of imagining*, that is, swift succession of one thought to another; and *steady direction* to some approved end'. Hobbes here seems not to have been thinking primarily of wit as laughable, but it was in that more modern sense of the word that he was most often quoted by the Victorians. In men's thoughts, Hobbes continues,

there is nothing to observe in the things they think on, but either in what they be *like one another*, or in what they be *unlike*, or *what they serve for*, or *how they serve to such a purpose*; those that observe their similitudes, in case they be such as are but rarely observed by others, are said to have a *good wit*; by which, in this occasion, is meant a *good fancy*. But they that observe their differences, and dissimilitudes; which is called *distinguishing*, and *discerning*, and *judging* between thing and thing; in case, such discerning be not easy, are said to have a *good judgment* . . .

Hobbes left little doubt where his own choice lay between these two intellectual virtues, for 'without steadiness, and direction to some end, a great fancy is one kind of madness'. In good poems, he admits, 'both judgment and fancy are required: but the fancy must be more eminent; because they please for the extravagancy; but ought not to displease by indiscretion'.

On the other hand, in a good history, which is the province of judgement, 'Fancy has no place, but only in adorning the style.'

The sense of wit as laughable is suggested when Hobbes considers the 'passion that hath *no name*' that results in both laughter and joy: 'That it consisteth in *wit*, or, as they call it, in the *jest*, experience *confuteth* . . .' When he is restating his theory of superiority, he writes that 'men laugh at *jests*, the *wit* whereof always consisteth in the elegant *discovering* and conveying to our minds some *absurdity* of *another* . . .' Again, he is obviously thinking of wit as risible when he warns against levity, 'an example whereof is in them that in the midst of any serious discourse, have their minds diverted to every little jest or witty observation'.[11]

It was, therefore, with considerable justification that the Victorians so often referred to Hobbes for authority in the disapproval of laughter and of wit (which is conducive to laughter). The same case was put more memorably, and more condescendingly, by Locke in *An Essay Concerning Human Understanding*. 'Quickness of parts' consists of having ideas ready at hand, judgement consists of 'being able nicely to distinguish one thing from another'. That, he continues, is why

men who have a great deal of wit, and prompt memories, have not always the clearest judgment or deepest reason. For *wit* lying most in the assemblage of ideas, and putting those together with quickness and variety, wherein can be found any resemblance or congruity, thereby to make up pleasant pictures and agreeable visions in the fancy; *judgment*, on the contrary, lies quite on the other side, in separating carefully, one from another, ideas wherein can be found the least difference, thereby to avoid being misled by similitude, and by affinity to take one thing for another.

The meaning Locke is attaching to wit is still in a state of transition, even half a century after Hobbes, for he clearly means by it both that which causes laughter because of its verbal and mental ingenuity, and pure ingenuity unconnected with laughter. And in neither case does it rise above a mere agglomeration. In some of the hardest words ever written about wit, he stresses the lack of necessity of mental exertion to respond to such ingenuity. Judgement, he says, is

quite contrary to metaphor and allusion, wherein for the most part lies that entertainment and pleasantry of wit, which strikes so lively on the fancy, and therefore is so acceptable to all people, because its beauty appears at first sight, and there is required no labour of thought to examine what truth or reason there is in it. The mind, without looking any further, rests satisfied with the agreeableness of the picture and the gaiety of the fancy. And it is a kind of affront to go about to examine it, by the severe rules of truth and good reason; whereby it appears that it consists in something that is not perfectly conformable to them.[12]

For Hobbes and Locke the equation of wit with fancy probably meant primarily that wit was capricious, arbitrary, fictive —in brief, fanciful. By the nineteenth century the meaning of fancy had undergone a slight modification, and it now referred chiefly to the ability to juxtapose objects, ideas, or images on the basis of a very incomplete likeness, the contemplation of which did not lead to further illumination of the parts being compared. It depended upon a kind of memory based on incomplete association. Because the association was on the surface and partial, the comparison was arbitrary, since the terms of likeness did not refer to the essence of either of the two parts of the comparison. In Coleridge's thinking, for example, fancy was like an arbitrary simile, while in contrast the imagination was like a symbol, the contemplation of whose meaning was a constantly expanding process. What is common to Hobbes and Locke on one side and the Victorians on the other in their consideration of the fancy is that it is for both—but for very different reasons—an inferior mode of perception. Indeed, it might be said that it was inferior for Hobbes because it was poetic in nature, for the Victorians because it was only a low form of the poetic, and hence not truly poetic, as they thought of the term. Whatever its meaning, the term had become opprobrious, and hence its constant employment in reference to wit is an indication of the triviality which was ascribed to that faculty by much of the nineteenth century.

In Romantic (and much of Victorian) theory the imagination was that total engagement of both emotion and intellect that transcended either of them alone; in practice the emotions were accorded a considerable precedence over the intellect. Since wit was inextricably linked with the intellect, it seemed distinctly inferior to humour proceeding from the emotions. Furthermore, it was obvious that the sympathy which informed humour was denied to wit, which therefore had to be cold, even cynical. Wit was generally conceded to be something that entertained by virtue of the surprise inherent in the linking of the fundamentally incompatible, and since surprise is necessarily transitory, wit is no more than—literally—passing fancy. There is no meat, no sustenance in it, as there is in humour, which nourishes both observed and observer. Wit 'elicits only the silent smile of the intellect', said a reviewer in 1822; 'on which account (whatever my writings may testify to the contrary) I have no great regard for wit, for I love to laugh with all my heart and none of my head'.[13] The statement might have stood without emendation for an entire generation.

One of the aspects of wit that often came in for hard knocks was the play upon words. A *Westminster* reviewer of 1871 spoke of 'the evanescent character of wit, and especially that form of wit we call "punning". A flash, a sudden contrast, a laugh, and all is over; the heartiness of our laughter being in proportion to our surprise, and we can only be surprised once.' The attitude was one that had occurred long before and has surprisingly persisted into our own century. Harold Nicolson, for example, discounted word-play, since 'no mental effort is needed or attempted; the reaction is, if not entirely physiological, is [*sic*] certainly not one by which the higher cortices of the brain are affected. It is thus a primal, or infantile, reaction.'*

Humour was linked with the roots of a whole people. It was 'their institutions, laws, customs, manners, habits, characters, convictions,—their scenery, whether of the sea, the city, or the hills,—expressed in the language of the ludicrous, uttering themselves in the tones of genuine and heartfelt mirth'.[14] And nowhere was humour so well understood as in England. It was generally accepted that humour was traditionally English, so indigenous to Anglo-Saxon and Teutonic peoples that it was

* [J. Fraser?], 'Thomas Hood', *Westminster Review* XXXIX, n.s. (April 1871), 348; Nicolson, *The English Sense of Humour and Other Essays* (1956), p. 40. The latter work, which is highly derivative from James Sully and Alexander Bain, is valuable as an example of how little effect the work of critics, philosophers, and psychologists may have on succeeding popularizers. For example, Nicolson writes that 'it will be agreed that the essential difference between humour and wit is that, whereas wit is always intentional, humour is always unintentional' (p. 18).

useless to attempt to translate either the term or the practice into a Latin tongue. In England 'humour is the chief expression of jocularity. . . . broad, genial, glorious humour. . . . When it becomes forked with sarcasm, and takes to riving hearts of oak, and tearing off the roof of men's houses, and shaking down steeples, then it is not true English humour.'[15]

Wit, on the other hand, dealt with abstract matters and was essentially foreign. To a reviewer in the *British Quarterly Review* it was 'the distinctive feature of the French genius, and humour of the English'.[16]* Not infrequently wit was allowed to the Irish, and Americans were conceded to have humour, however exaggerated it might be, but this was largely because they were of English stock.

Gerald Massey even gave democratic reasons for the superiority of humour to wit: it has a wider range and hence can appeal to the uneducated. It contents the heart, while wit only teases. It is the comfort of the domestic fire on the hearth, while wit is only a spark that is gone in a moment leaving neither light nor heat. 'Wit is more artificial, and a thing of culture; humour lies nearer to nature.'[17]

Wit 'sweetened by a kind, loving expression, becomes Humour', the *Westminster* said in 1847. Leigh Hunt, sitting uncomfortably on the fence between wit and humour, characteristically paid tribute to both, then decided that wit alone 'is but an element for professors to sport with'. Only when it is combined with humour does it run 'into the richest utility' and help 'to humanize the world'. John Morley said that Byron 'was full not merely of wit, which is sometimes only an affair of the tongue, but of humour also, which goes deeper' and 'binds the thoughts of him who possesses it to the wide medley of expressly human things'. To Walter Pater wit was 'that unreal and transitory mirth which is as the crackling of thorns under the pot', while humour was 'the laughter which blends

---

* Harold Nicolson believed that true English humour is good-natured, and that 'derisive laughter has little to do with the English sense of humour' (*The English Sense of Humour*, p. 11). The statement quite properly excludes such Irishmen as Wilde and Shaw and Joyce, but it is hard to see how he could have believed it after reading Ronald Firbank or Evelyn Waugh or Ivy Compton-Burnett, to name only three novelists writing during his own maturity who were apparently untainted by foreign blood.

with tears and even with the subtleties of the imagination, and which, in its most exquisite motives, is one with pity . . .'[18]

Pater's mention of imagination may remind us that humour was traditionally connected with it, and that wit, as Hobbes and Locke had both assumed, was a product of the fancy. It was a distinction that echoed through the nineteenth century, often without much examination of what was meant by the words used. 'Wit, in its way of working, is akin to Fancy', according to Massey. 'But Humour is allied to the greatness and oneness of Imagination.' In the *Dublin University Magazine* T. C. Irwin wrote that wit consists of 'coldly brilliant displays of pure intellect, whose combinations serve to awaken laughter merely'. The highest form to which wit could aspire was 'the united product of fancy and analogy, or of the reason and fancy'. It is an echo of Coleridge, finding to his dismay that 'it is not always easy to distinguish between wit and fancy'.[19]

The distinction between fancy and imagination was a standard one in the nineteenth century to apply to the difference between prose and poetry. Since wit was connected with the fancy, it became linked with prose; humour, because of its connection with the imagination, naturally became attached to poetry. 'The peculiar nineteenth-century emphasis on its sympathy immediately placed humour in a realm of emotion as opposed to dead abstraction, of value as opposed to fact, in the realm, in short, in which poetry also resided.'[20]

Carlyle had made the same distinction in 1829 when he wrote that Voltaire's wit 'stands related to Humour as Prose does to Poetry'. George Eliot, who by no means despised the intellect as Carlyle did, said that humour 'has more affinity with the poetic tendencies' than wit, which 'is more nearly allied to the ratiocinative intellect'. Humour 'continually passes into poetry'.[21]

Once more, it is difficult to penetrate the customary speech and assumptions of the Victorians to see precisely what Carlyle (and probably George Eliot) intended. They were, in the first place, presumably suggesting that humour, reflective of the imagination, was the more creative form of comedy, penetrating much more deeply than wit into the meaning of the subjects that it considered. But there is, even in the best of writers, a frequent usage of terms whose residual meanings remain unexamined. Probably Carlyle and George Eliot also credited humour with poetic powers simply because poetry was generally accepted by their contemporaries to be superior to prose; in part their words may have been vague encomia, signifying little more than the attribution of nobility to humour would have done. Certainly the audience for whom they were writing would have taken 'poetic' as complimentary rather than analytical. The fact remains that humour was still generally regarded as the higher of the two manifestations of the comic spirit.

Humour had nearly total sway in the nineteenth century until the late 1860s, when we find the reviewers and critics becoming increasingly restive about the state of comic writing. Wit and intellectual comedy had been universally agreed upon as arrogant, cold, and unpoetic, but when they had almost disappeared in practice, the suspicion grew that they might be a cool refreshment from the sticky and unrelieved sentimentality of what had been passing as comedy.

At first most of the criticism concentrated on the stage. When laughter had been removed as a criterion of comedy, the gates had been opened to almost any kind of representation that would arouse easy emotion. Once French theatre had seemed the essence of heartlessness; now there was a nagging worry that its intellectual tradition might be more acceptable to intelligent men than the debased spectacles of the London stage. The last great comic writer for the English stage had been Sheridan, a century before—and he was Irish. For half that time he had been a byword for heartless brilliance, now he began to seem a figure from a remote and golden age: 'like that of Chivalry, the age of Comedy is past', a writer in the *Broadway* said in 1869, lamenting the quality of Sheridan's successors.[22]

Percy Fitzgerald wrote *Principles of Comedy and Dramatic Effect*, a very long book indeed, to indicate the low estate into which the English stage had fallen in 1870. The follies and eccentricities that had once formed the substance of serious comedy had become so overdrawn that there was no longer any comic effect produced. The only successful 'sparkling' or 'epigrammatic' comedies were French in origin and tailored for the London stage by a whole 'adapting trade' busy at stealing from across the Channel. All that the native writers could produce was increasingly mechanical spectacle that went by the name of comedy. 'A tree that bent over a precipice (bent, too, by means of a very palpable hinge): the slow rising of water in a cave, a house on fire, a tunnel and locomotive, some vulgar slang songs, a steamboat—these are the triumphs on which we plume ourselves.' Fitzgerald was something of a hack and his book a vulgar and over-extended patchwork, but his very lack of originality is indicative of the widespread discontent that he voiced. Perhaps most telling of all is the acknowledgement that English writers might have something to learn from the French.[23]

But it was not stage comedy alone that came in for heavy strictures. The proliferation of 'comic' papers had been the subject of complaint by an anonymous writer in *Temple Bar* in 1863, and the examples that he offered are sufficiently appalling to prove his contention. The 'wit, humour, and pointed sarcasm' of an earlier age were gone, and all that was left was vulgar and outrageous.[24] There is what seems almost a conspiracy nowadays to find *Punch* of the mid-nineteenth century penetratingly amusing, but it is an attitude that is scarcely supported by reading the issues of the 1850s and 1860s. What seems sadly lacking is precisely the wit, humour, and point that the *Temple Bar* writer regretted, and what it offers instead is comfort and reinforcement to middle-class prejudices.*

An amusing outsider's view of English comedy is provided by Hippolyte Taine, whose *History of English Literature* was published in four stout volumes in 1874, just at the time that the English themselves were becoming aware of deficiencies in contemporary comedy. With Gallic disdain for what had been proceeding in the British Isles for a century, Taine says of Carlyle that his 'kind of mind produces humour, a word untranslatable in French, because in France they have not the idea. Humour is a species of talent which amuses Germans, Northmen; it suits their mind, as beer and brandy suit their palate.' What there is of English wit 'consists of saying very

---

* An exaggerated complaint that *Punch*, 'once the Glory of periodical literature and which is now its Shame', had sunk to mere anti-Catholicism was made by [Thomas Donnelly], 'Modern Humorists', *Dublin Review*, XLVIII (May 1860), 149.

jocular things in a solemn manner', but the jocularity is assumed, since the chief element of the English character is 'its want of happiness'. When one attempts to amuse the English, their 'immobile and contracted faces will preserve the same attitude', and they resist the temptation to smile. The truth is that 'they cannot unbend; and their laughter is a convulsion as stiff as their gravity'.

Taine is no more fair to English writers than English critics were to the comic writers of other nationalities, but his is a refreshingly different point of view. English society seems a natural subject for comedy, since it is 'a compound of flatteries and intrigues, each striving to hoist himself up a step higher on the social ladder and to push back those who are climbing'. But one dare not touch 'the smallest moral conventionalism', for, no matter how carefully it is done, 'immediately fifty hands will fasten themselves on our coat collar and put us out at the door.' The result is that there is no true comedy, and the novel of manners

multiplies, and for this there are several reasons: first, it is born there, and every plant thrives well in its own soil; secondly, it is a natural outlet: there is no music in England as in Germany or conversation as in France; and men who must think and feel find in it a means of feeling and thinking. On the other hand, women take part in it with eagerness; amidst the stagnation of gallantry and the coldness of religion, it gives scope for imagination and dreams. Finally, by its minute details and practical counsels, it opens up a career to the precise and moral mind.

Over and over Taine makes the point that the English have developed their own peculiar forms of comedy because they are afraid of enjoyment; what they really believe in is the punitive aspect of comedy, and it is because of this deep belief in a form of literature from which they cannot help shrinking in re-pugnance, that they are unable to take joy in wit and the intellect. Even when they think they are being humorous and loving, they are finally committed to ridicule. 'Feeling pain-fully all the wrongs that are committed, and the vices that are practised, Dickens avenges himself by ridicule. He does not paint, he punishes.' Of the novel of manners, Taine says that the 'lash is laid on very heavily in this school; it is the English

taste'. Among all satirists, 'Thackeray, after Swift, is the most
gloomy'.[25]

The importance of Taine's strictures is that they make explicit from the outside what had been disturbing the most
thoughtful of English critics.

The same year Frank Penthorne published an article on
comedy in *Belgravia*; most of it is little more than rhetorical
gush, but he does indicate a change of attitude towards the
utility of comedy that depended upon incongruity for its being.
Even the most tragic natures, he thought, usually have an
element of comedy 'which enables a man in hours of depression
to regard things from a ludicrous point of view, and to extract
matter of merriment from his very misfortunes'; this 'is more
valuable than the profoundest teachings of philosophy in
qualifying him to endure with equanimity the troubles and
tribulations of life'. As a definition of the uses of comedy this
defence is perhaps not much more valuable than earlier ones
that had said it was good for the spleen or the liver or in the
prevention of apoplexy, but it does point towards a more
general acceptance of comedy and thus the necessity of defining
its utility. Even such ladies' groups as the 'Victoria Discussion
Society' were arguing the subject; on 6 May 1874 'Mr. Serjeant
Cox read the . . . paper on "Wit and Humour" ' to the Society
in the Cavendish Rooms. His formulations were traditional,
the demand for popular discussion of them was new.[26]

Gerald Massey, as we have seen, in 1860 had praised humour
over wit because it was more available to the uneducated. Only
three years later the same premise was used for an opposite
conclusion when the *Westminster* said that it 'implies some talent
and quickness to appreciate a witticism, but the lower kinds of
humour are capable of such marked demonstration that they
may be enjoyed, and are commonly most enjoyed, by the
vulgar and illiterate'. The entire *Westminster* article is written
in a curiously ambivalent fashion, on one side clearly worrying
about the limits of subject that must be prescribed for comedy,
on the other fretting about the inadequacy of humour and wit
as they had been conceived of for generations.[27]

Obviously, the critical definition of comedy and the measurement of its utility had a limited appeal to the reading public,
and none but the most zealous of historians could believe that

they were burning issues, in spite of the frequency with which the subject crops up in Victorian periodicals. To see changes in opinion clearly, we must telescope what took place over years and give a falsely linear quality to what was actually a jerky, back-and-forth movement. The reviewer in the *British Quarterly Review* who in 1870 had remarked that humour merited repeated study while wit did not, called wit 'an operation of pure intellect' which 'when most brilliant is by no means provocative of laughter'. It is instructive to see that wit is being dissociated from laughter, that old bugbear of which humour had to be purged in order to become respectable; however mistaken one may find the reasoning, this is part of the rehabilitation of wit, although that process was by no means yet complete. The article reflects nostalgia in the recognition that Dickens has swept all before him, and that wit has given way totally in the past to humour. None the less, the reviewer still feels that wit is contrived and laborious, that both wit and mathematics are 'enjoyable at fit times, and both have a tendency to tire'. It is improbable that the typical product of wit, the epigram, will ever be restored to public favour, for life 'is not long enough for the labour which good epigrams require'.

The article quotes Chesterfield's dictum that one should appear to have rather less wit than one really has, since a wise man will live at least as much within his wit as within his income. 'The advice is judicious,' the reviewer wryly remarks; 'but perhaps it is not important to enforce it in an age when wit is somewhat at a discount.'[28]

In 1872, only two years after this review, another article in the *British Quarterly Review* showed the changes that were already overtaking the consideration of wit. There is no indication that the articles were written by the same person, but it is at least remarkable that two articles so different should have appeared in the same magazine. The second of these writers quotes from the review of Leigh Hunt's book in the *Westminster* of 1847, in order to justify his own mixed feelings about wit and humour. 'There are few greater mistakes than the supposition that wit is frivolous,' the writer says in direct contradiction to the majority of previous criticism in the century. Though humour requires a good heart, 'wit requires a good head'. It 'need not always be ludicrous or laughable; in fact, we think it may sometimes be serious, but it must not be too heavily loaded'.

There is a token nod in the direction of the superiority of humour, which is acknowledged to be 'a higher, finer, and more genial thing', since unadulterated wit 'is often ill-natured, and has a sting', but the fact that wit is 'more allied to intellect' does not necessarily make its laughter more arrogant or bitter than that of humour.

Most of the philosophers who have set to work to define mental sensations insist that laughter supposes a feeling of superiority in the laugher over the laughed at; but they seem to overlook the great distinction between laughing at and laughing with any one. Doubtless a feeling of contempt often raises a laugh, and the absurdities of men and women are a constant food for laughter; but humourists often laugh at themselves.

The true result of wit is pleasure, for the only constant effect following 'on an original and striking comparison is a shock of agreeable surprise; it is as if a partition-wall in our intellect was suddenly blown out; two things formerly strange to one another have flashed together'.

Perhaps the ideas advanced here seem less than startling, but they are indicative of a big change in thinking about comedy. In theories of 'amiable' humour the assumption was that emotion (humour) was warm, intellect (wit) was cold, apparently without recognition that coldness is as emotional as warmth, and that the imputation of it to intellect is in itself a judgement by the emotions. So long as one insisted on thinking in terms of emotion, it was impossible to recognize the claims of the intellect. What the 1872 reviewer is stating is that comedy need be neither warm nor cold, neither sympathetic nor hostile: the pleasures of the intellect may arise simply from the recognition of heightened awareness.

It is tempting to give too much weight to the article, to read into it an approbation of wit and intellectual comedy that the reviewer did not intend. It would be difficult, however, to overstate the importance of the reviewer's definition of wit as 'often little more than the unused side of wisdom, which commonplace people do not see . . . the highest wit is wisdom at play'.[29] It is a formulation that indicates an attitude to comedy that had not been widely accepted in comic theory for a century, and that had not often been apparent in practice except in the novels of Jane Austen and Peacock. George Meredith's particular form of comedy had been in part evident in such works as *Richard Feverel*, *Evan Harrington*, or *Harry Richmond*, and—perhaps most characteristically—in the peculiar comic highlights of his 'tragic' poem *Modern Love*.

In April 1871 Charles Cowden Clarke began a series oi fifteen articles 'On the Comic Writers of England' that appeared at monthly intervals in the *Gentleman's Magazine*; the fact that so many long articles (normally of twenty to twenty-five pages) were published on the subject is indication of the interest in it that editors must have sensed in the reading public. Clarke accepted without examination the premise that comedy may be impersonal, neither sympathetic nor antagonistic, a view that is in itself a long way from the older ideas about humour. Wit consists 'in exposing, and holding up to ridicule the unconsciously ludicrous in a principle, or an individual'. Humour is 'a graphically surcharged portraiture of the ludicrous position itself of the principle, or individual'. The phrasing of the distinction is unclear, but apparently he is suggesting that wit deals with ideas and with the abstract, while humour is the illustration or delineation of those ideas. The distinction is made clearer when he says that wit is superior to humour because it is 'the offspring of the inventive faculty, as well as of the imagination, and the fancy'. In other words, wit is the expression of the totality of the human powers. Even the pun, which had had to skulk like a pariah around the fringes of comedy, is recognized for its potentiality; 'no man ever despised a pun who could make one', wrote Clarke with admirable brevity. The critical statement of the relationship between wit and humour has come full circle.[30]

The last example of the consideration of wit and humour before turning to more major writers of the period comes from Isaac Tuxton, writing in the *Irish Monthly* in 1877, the year when Meredith spoke on the Comic Spirit. Tuxton's work is a mixture of shrewdness and dull schoolmasterly platitude; what is interesting is that it is surprisingly advanced in its conception of wit, not only as a product of the intellect but also as a legitimate form of knowledge.

Tuxton begins with the standard, Lockeian idea of wit as the 'assemblage of ideas' on the basis of their likeness. But Hobbes and Locke and their British successors of the first three quarters of the nineteenth century had thought of the assemblage as being the artificial linking of the fundamentally incompatible; for them the pleasure of wit lay in the surprise of the yoking of the essentially incongruous. Tuxton, however, grasped the basic principle of good wit as being that which reveals, in a paradoxical manner, the real congruity of two or more terms which seem at first sight to be incompatible; if there is not a flash of recognition of the real fitness of the assemblage, then the wit is ephemeral. The flash of recognition produces laughter from the fresh knowledge of 'relational ideas', and beyond the laughter is the sense of having learned something about a pattern which links separate elements of the world of ideas. It is basically the method of poetry, and this Tuxton realized:

> The mental power of the poet, orator, literateur, and wit, for perceiving rare, delicate, real, superficial resemblances, links, or relations, between ideas of things apparently the most remote from one another, is one and the same. However, the phenomena of this power, which provoke smiles and laughter, are alone commonly called wit. They are distinguished from the other phenomena of the same faculty . . . in that they produce admiration of, and sympathy with, the agent . . . together with a feeling of superiority of some kind in the percipient, and the surprise, admiration, sympathy, and self-satisfaction are expressed by delighted smiles and laughter.

This is to postulate a meaning for wit that extends far beyond that of surface amusement. 'Wherever resemblances or relations are established between ideas, knowledge of some sort is communicated,' Tuxton says astutely. 'Wit establishes such relations. . . . Therefore wit is knowledge, and communicates knowledge.' Humour, rather than being the paramount form of the ludicrous, is only a form of wit, 'the wit of the emotions or feelings . . . the fusion of contrasted emotions'.[31]

What has been provided is a rationale for the great tradition of writers in the English language who have used intellectual comedy as a method of investigating the meaning of the world about them. Congreve, Sterne, Swift, Jane Austen, and Peacock, to name only a few, have been of that company before the period we have been examining. It is at least arguable that the real glory of English literature since 1877 has been the product of the great witty writers: Meredith, Butler, Wilde, Shaw in the last century; Firbank, Huxley, Waugh, Ivy Compton-Burnett in our own; and possibly Graham Greene, Muriel Spark, Angus Wilson, Anthony Powell, Elizabeth Bowen, and Iris Murdoch as well. Critics tend to overemphasize the importance of theory, I realize, but it is none the less chastening to realize that had there been a continuation of the tradition that produced Dickens (and much of Thackeray and Trollope), there would have been little place for the witty writers I have mentioned. Without the change in theory, the practice of English literature might have been a different and, probably, a poorer thing.

## CHAPTER IV

# Phrenological Formulations

IMPROBABLY enough, from the 1820s to the early 1840s some of the most spirited discussion of comic theory came out of one of the obscure but not unimportant intellectual offshoots of the period, the new 'science' of phrenology, which is probably more familiar to the twentieth century as a butt of comedy than as a source of speculation about comic theory. Like most other schools of thought, phrenology had to reformulate traditional problems in its own language, and in the process of translation had to rethink the problems. Today its notions about comedy are more important as indications of contemporary ideas on the subject than as original contributions to theory.

Phrenology was essentially German and Austrian in origin, moved to France and England, and finally found its most widespread acceptance in the United States, where it persisted well into this century, as it has in England, where there is still an intermittent trickle of books on the subject.

Franz Joseph Gall, born in Baden, near Pforzheim, in 1758, began writing on phrenology in 1798, and by 1802 had commanded such a following in Austria that the government commanded him to discontinue lecturing on the subject because the Church believed that he was endangering orthodox religion. Most of his subsequent writing and teaching was done in Paris. His outstanding pupil was Johann Gaspar Spurzheim from near Trier, who became his disciple in 1800. Spurzheim, who disagreed on some points with his master, was largely responsible for the spread of phrenology in Great Britain and the United States, where he died in 1832, only two years after Gall's death. The speed with which Spurzheim's doctrines were disseminated is indicated by the disapproving words of one Scotsman who remained unconverted, Thomas Carlyle: 'Such is the order of Nature: a Spurzheim flies from Vienna to Paris and London within the year; a Kant, slowly advancing, may perhaps reach us from Königsberg within the century . . .'[1]

Phrenology (which was also known as cranioscopy, craniology, physiognomy, and zoonomy) was an early and serious attempt to discover the functions of the various parts of the brain, but it has more often been remembered for the wilder reaches of its application than for its genuine search for knowledge. Gall and Spurzheim and their followers held to the principle that the mind is composed of a number of independent faculties, each of which has a definite region in the surface of the brain. Those regions, or 'organs', of the brain in turn influence the shape of the head, and examination of the external surface of the head allows the observer to recognize the relative size of the organs inside. When he knows both the location of the organ and its size and development, he can make a postulation about the quality of the mind and potentialities of the subject. It is this last, the 'reading of bumps', later carried on as a public entertainment like hypnotism and palmistry, which brought phrenology into popular disrepute, long after it had been rejected by most scientists. Gall listed twenty-six organs, and other phrenologists claimed to have identified as many as forty-three. For our purposes the three most important were those known as the organs of Causality, Secretiveness, and Wit (or *esprit caustique*, as Gall named it). Before Gall first published his findings in 1798, 'the whole discoveries were little more than the coincidences of particular local protuberances of the cranium with particular dispositions or talents', according to Hewett Watson. 'It was several years later that the united abilities of Gall and Spurzheim—more especially the latter—systematized their discoveries into a connected outline of the science as now known.'[2]

It was in Edinburgh that both the enemies of phrenology and its defenders were found in greatest strength. The *Edinburgh Review*, chiefly at the instigation of Jeffrey, had begun attacking it early in the century, and in 1806 the *Edinburgh Medical and Surgical Journal* carried an unflattering notice of Gall.[3] Spurzheim made his first visit to England in 1814 and published *The Physiognomical System of Drs Gall and Spurzheim* the following year. When the *Edinburgh* attacked the book as quackery, Spurzheim went to Scotland for a series of lectures and for a public dissection of a brain as demonstration of the principles of phrenology. One of the audience was George

Combe, a barrister, who was 'converted' from Calvinism[4] and finally became the systematizer of phrenology, as Watson was its historian. With a few like-minded believers he founded the Phrenological Society of Edinburgh in 1820. It was, Watson wrote, 'the most memorable event in the history of phrenology, that had occurred since Spurzheim's visit to England and publication of the physiognomical System. This Society concentrated the strength of phrenologists into a citadel, as it were, within the very city where phrenology had been so hostilely opposed and so virulently abused.'[5]

It was perhaps the same quality inherent in phrenology that had been responsible for the banning of Gall's lectures in Vienna which led to its becoming so firmly rooted in Edinburgh. The Catholic authorities in Austria had been afraid that the location of the source of behaviour and personality in inherited organs of the brain would lead to the destruction of belief in free will. For Calvinist Scots the attribution of the source of character to bumps on the head may have been pleasanter than accepting predestination, although they perhaps came to the same thing in the end. In any case, the first quarterly number of *The Phrenological Journal and Miscellany* appeared in 1823. It was destined to run to twenty volumes (with a change of title to *The Phrenological Journal and Magazine of Moral Science* after the first ten) before it ceased publication in 1847. 'It has never been very popular, even among the phrenologists,' Watson confessed,* but during its publication its contributors frequently speculated about wit, humour, and laughter; in part they were concerned with the location of the organs themselves and with their specific functions, but to decide the answers to these questions they frequently involved themselves with the older ones about the quality and nature of wit and humour. The history of the discussion of such

---

* *Statistics of Phrenology* (1836), p. 14. Watson, who was a distinguished naturalist, was a fierce controversialist and frequent contributor to the first series of the *Phrenological Journal*. In 1837 he bought its copyright, changed its title, and served as unpaid editor until 1840. At that time, after quarreling in print with many of his fellow phrenologists, he left the movement, although he is said to have continued his belief in its general principles. His 'Introductory Explanation to the New Series' (XI, 1–12) indicates that he took over a large debt with the journal and had no hope of making money from it.

philosophical questions is usually one of changing terms not of new basic conceptions, and the framework of phrenology gave fresh impetus to the discussion. After all, it meant much the same for a phrenologist to speak of a comic writer's being deficient in the organ of Veneration as it had when Hobbes said that wit was dependent upon feelings of superiority.

Wit and humour, however, have other manifestations than literature, and had the phrenologists been interested only in their appearance in, say, conversation of the style of Chesterfield or Wilde, their discussions would have been of little concern to anyone interested in comic writing. Their particular method of investigation of the functions of the various organs of the brain made it convenient for them to turn to comic literature. In general, they proceeded by first observing a large number of individuals who manifested the same trait, then attempting to see what phrenological development they had in common. In daily life this was not always easy, since no one investigator (and most of them were only part-time phrenologists who spent their days as barristers or doctors) was apt to know enough of the separate characters of a large group of persons to generalize about them. It was easier to turn to writers, who revealed their inner natures more clearly in their works than other persons did in their actions and conversation. Although it was seldom possible to proceed from the writer to a personal and minute examination of his cranial development, one could at least look at the plentiful examples of pictures, masks, and busts. The consequence is that in many of the discussions of the functions of the organ of Wit, the theory is advanced, then illustrated from the works of such writers as Chaucer, Shakespeare, Sterne, Congreve, Sheridan, Cervantes, and Rabelais, and finally, when possible, substantiated by reference to the authors' phrenological development as revealed in portraits. Not only were long-dead authors 'phrenologized'; even major fictional characters like Hamlet and Falstaff and Don Quixote were subjected to postulation about their necessary phrenological development. That such writers as Charlotte Brontë, George Eliot, and Bulwer-Lytton all used phrenology to indicate character is demonstration of the direct influence of phrenology on literature.

The phrenologists generally accepted the theory of incongruity to account for wit and comedy, although a number of them combined it with the theory of superiority.* Most of the discussion (and bitter dissension) came from a disagreement over the nature of wit: whether it sprang from the comparison of similarities, as Locke had insisted, or whether it was the result of the awareness of differences between two ideas.

Gall early observed that witty persons, fond of sprightly sallies and repartee 'have the upper and outer parts of the forehead, immediately before the organs of Ideality, much developed', and to that region he gave the name of *esprit caustique* or *esprit de saillie*. He attempted no analysis of the faculty and said that he could describe it no better than by saying that it was the quality most conspicuous in the writings of Rabelais, Cervantes, Swift, Sterne, and Voltaire. In his early writings Spurzheim named the faculty Wit, and said that its function consists 'in comparing objects in order to discover their similarity or dissimilarity . . . and comparing in a philosophical way is quite different from comparing wittily'. The peculiarity of its method of comparison is that it 'always excites gaiety and laughter'. In later editions of his *Physiognomical System* he classified wit as an emotion not an intellectual power. In short he was demoting wit from a method of thought to a generalized feeling which could be thrown over any intellectual activity to give it a particular colour, that of 'mirthfulness or gayness'.[6] It should be noticed, however, that he believed— not surprisingly—that mirth, wit, gaiety, and laughter were the products of the organ of Wit.

In a review of Spurzheim in 1824 the editor of the *Phrenological Journal* (presumably William Scott) stated that the finest specimens of wit 'often combine [perceptions of both resemblances and incongruities], and consist in discovering an unexpected resemblance amidst great seeming differences, or an unexpected difference where there is a great seeming resemblance'. In the most broadly ludicrous, 'the difference . . . is always more striking than the resemblance'. Therefore, according to the author of the review, it was apparent that the

---

* That Gall called the organ of Wit the *esprit caustique* is sufficient indication that the theory of superiority was influential among the early phenologists. English and Scottish phrenologists, however, leaned heavily towards the theory of incongruity.

E

most important function of the organ of Wit 'is the *perception of differences*, and that wit, or the feeling of the ludicrous, is only one of the results of this faculty when in its most active state'.*

Scott's major consideration of the subject under his own name was in 1827, in an essay called 'Of Wit and the Feeling of the Ludicrous', in which he set out to restore wit as an intellectual power. Much of the phrenologists' consideration of the subject for the next two decades was prompted by this essay.

For Scott the study of wit begins with the tacit assumption of incongruity as the cause of laughter, although 'various theories have been proposed'. By the time he wrote it was 'generally admitted that it is caused by some kind of incongruity' (IV, 196). Also he accepts without examination the premise that wit is allied to laughter.

Where Spurzheim seems to have taken his idea of wit from Locke, Scott begins, like a good Scot, by invoking James Beattie, author of *Essay on Laughter and Ludicrous Composition* (1776) and Alexander Gerard, *Essay on Taste* (1759), to confirm the theory of incongruity. Then he turns to the examination of 'four species of incongruity', which Beattie says 'excite the feeling of the ludicrous' (IV, 197). Scott's essay is long and sometimes rambling, but there are a number of excellent observations made in its course.

Beattie had said that one cause of laughter is the result of 'incongruous particulars . . . united by mere juxta-position' (IV, 197). Scott realized that there must be more connection and association between the particulars than Beattie had suggested, that to produce an effect there must be a bond of union among them, and he prefers the word 'grouping' to that of 'juxta-position' (IV, 199). The contrast between 'short, tall, fat, and lean people in a public street' (IV, 198) does not produce laughter, but the sight of 'a tall awkward woman stooping down to the arm of a little purfled round-bellied mannikin whom she could apparently carry in her pocket' (IV, 197) is ludicrous because the disparity occurs within an implied

---

* 'Dr Spurzheim's French Works', II, 197. Scott, a lawyer, was one of the original proprietors of the *Journal*, but within a few years he withdrew from all connection with it. It seems probable that he was the author of the Spurzheim review, since he was one of the editors and since both the views and phraseology are like his later writings.

bond. What is implicit in Scott's statement is that there must be both comparison and contrast for incongruity to have its effect. When this condition is fulfilled, 'the laughable effect seems . . . to be in proportion to the greatness of the contrast . . .' (IV, 198). Elsewhere he remarks that in examples of the highly ludicrous, 'the contrast cannot fail to strike every one as far more remarkable than the resemblance'. When two objects excite precisely opposite feelings on being put into a grouping,

in the instances of serious wit, we think chiefly of the *resemblance*, and the difference, though sufficiently obvious, is not dwelt upon; it occurs only so far as to give a sort of relief to the resemblance, and to occasion that pleasing surprise at its discovery which this species of wit excites. But in the ludicrous simile the resemblance is merely a sort of hook and eye to tie two things together which are the most opposite in nature. What strikes us most here is the *difference*, and though surprised certainly at the discovery of a resemblance between two things so prodigiously unlike, it is the contrast that chiefly occupies our attention; and it is this, as appears to me, which is the cause of our laughter (IV, 206–7).

Scott pursues his point through puns, 'where there is no resemblance whatever in the things themselves, but only in the sound of the words by which they are designated', and where the ludicrous effect is in 'exact proportion to the *contrast* between the ideas . . .' Similarly, when there is a patent absurdity in an assumed cause-and-effect, as when the fly on the chariot-wheel congratulates himself on the dust he is raising, the effect is dependent upon the enormity of the contrast (IV, 208–10).

He then turns to modes of writing, and he shows that the same rule for the ludicrous is applicable for burlesque (where 'dignified persons and actions are purposely degraded by vulgar language and mean circumstances') and travesty ('where the subject of a grave or elegant poem, or composition of any kind, is . . . related in low and colloquial language, in place of the high-sounding and poetical phrase which adorns the original'). Not only does our pleasure in these forms depend upon the vast difference between dignity and vulgarity, but the same contrast is observable in their mirror-forms, the mock-heroic ('vulgar thoughts are clothed in . . . the most inflated diction')

and parody ('ridiculous imitation of some well-known composition') (IV, 216–18).

As he continues his case, Scott cites Cervantes, whose story of
the Knight and the Squire teems 'with contrasts broad, palpable, and extravagant' (IV, 221). So far the argument is one
of repetition of example, but when he turns to Rabelais, Scott
unobtrusively brings in another approach to the ludicrous,
turning from the mind and phrenological development of the
writer to that of the reader or spectator. Clearly, Scott finds
himself out of sympathy with Rabelais, and he suggests that
his works cannot 'be properly enjoyed by any who do not
possess a development somewhat resembling that of the
author' (IV, 224). The suggestion that the material of wit and
the ludicrous is not necessarily inherently funny, but is dependent upon the cast of mind of the reader is not new, of
course, but it is a consideration of one aspect of the whole
subject that is seldom taken up in the nineteenth-century
theories of comedy and wit.

Swift, Sterne, Shakespeare, and Voltaire are all shown to
possess 'love of *contrast*' that is dependent upon 'a great development of the organ 32', and he concludes the first part of his
essay 'satisfied that contrast lies at the bottom of all' (IV, 229).

Scott's argument is coherent, although it does not seem to
account for all forms of the ludicrous. To make it more binding,
he turns back to the subject that had attracted his momentary
attention, laughter itself, rather than the ludicrous or laughable. He is prepared to assert that 'the *feeling* of the ludicrous,
and . . . that pleasing convulsion of the *faculties* called *laughter*'
are not more than incidentally connected with the organ of
Wit. 'The heartiest, the loudest, and the longest-continued
laughter is neither produced by any species of Wit, nor is the
indulgence of it confined to those in whom Wit is predominant.'
Swift, for example, 'seldom or never laughed' (IV, 230).

All the same, laughter is dependent upon contrast, precisely as wit is. The contrast, however, is between higher
emotions or 'intellectual powers' and the feelings that result
from the '*lower* propensities'. When a 'not much-displeased
damsel' is running away from a young man who wants to kiss
her, she laughs because 'the lower propensities would say *yes*,
the higher say *no*'. Boys 'and *Irishmen*' laugh at a comparatively

trivial misfortune to others; the delight arises from the jarring between the organ of Benevolence and those of Combativeness or Destructiveness (IV, 230–1).

Scott is apparently the first phrenologist to insist that the organ of Secretiveness is important in a sense of humour, for one must delight in maintaining gravity while saying that which provokes laughter in others. Clearly, for Scott the organ of Secretiveness implies some feelings of superiority over those whom the humourist is duping, although he does not directly condemn wit for that reason. Elsewhere he suggests that secretiveness is the quality responsible for creating plot in fiction because it lies behind surprise.[7] But one might remember, too, that it was generally credited by other phrenologists with being the main source not only of such admirable qualities as tact and reserve, but also of most secret crimes in the book, including blackmail and murder. Therefore, one is not surprised when laughter ultimately comes under Scott's censure.

'My theory, then,' he continues, 'is that laughter is occasioned by a slight degree of opposition between the *lower* propensities and the sentiments; and that, in the enjoyment which attends it, it is the former chiefly which are gratified, while the latter are always in some sort opposed to it' (IV, 236).

Cheerfulness, he says in an echo of the eighteenth century, should be 'the permanent habit of the mind, and mirth only an occasional indulgence'. He denies that he is so puritanical as to say that mirth, 'when kept within due bounds', is blameworthy, 'but with those who pursue it too eagerly, it may be extremely difficult so to restrain it'. The difficulty is that the lower propensities, however natural, break from under the control of the higher sentiments when they are 'indulged too eagerly or too long'. 'Fools are more addicted to laughter than wise men. Those in whom the higher sentiments predominate greatly over the propensities seldom laugh' (IV, 237–8). And, though we may speak of demoniac laughter, we do not speak of laughter of 'angels or glorified spirits' (IV, 240).

What is important theoretically to Scott about all this is that there is constant contrast between higher and lower feelings. It is 'the existence of opposite emotions, or, to speak phrenologically, the activity of opposite sets of faculties at the same time, that we have . . . come to consider to be the cause of laughter'. His conclusion, then, is that laughter results from *'contrasted feelings'*, and that a faculty which 'presents the mind with *contrasts'* is best calculated to produce ludicrous combinations. And that is what he has previously demonstrated is the function of 'organ 32'. Therefore, not only is contrast the essence of wit and laughter; it is also the function of the organ of Wit (IV, 241).

The essay and argument are ingenious. What must interest non-phrenologists most is the fact that it begins with a phrenological problem and finishes with an assertion of a solution to that problem, but during most of its course is dependent upon non-phrenological example and observation for its advancement.

For all its ingenuity and fundamental common sense, one cannot help feeling that the essay fails to recognize a real discrepancy between the theory of artistic creation and that of response to the work. Scott acknowledges that wit, in its creative aspect, may involve many kinds of contrast, but he insists that laughter results from only one kind, that between the higher emotions and the lower propensities. This is a constricting view of the range of laughter; worse, it suggests that any other kind of wit and comedy is ineffectual in arousing laughter in reader or auditor.

Scott's article provoked a number of responses in the *Phrenological Journal* over the course of the next decade or so. George Hancock, in a 'Letter on the Functions of the Organs of Comparison and Wit' (IX [September 1835], 435–43), defended Scott's view of wit as dependent upon both discrimination and perception of resemblance. In ludicrous wit resemblance is actually weak, and the differences broadly marked and essential, but the reverse is true in poetic wit: in 'beautiful or sublime similies and metaphors, the resemblance is real and palpable' (IX, 439).

Almost inadvertently Hancock defends wit from the condemnation of Locke. Spurzheim had followed Locke in thinking that wit resulted from comparison, and with George Combe had asserted 'that the perception of a resemblance is the result of a lower, and that of a difference of a higher, degree of power and activity in each intellectual faculty. Colour, for example, when feeble, *sees* a resemblance between hues, which, by a more powerful organ, are at once perceived to be different' (IX, 435). Hancock points out that it is impossible to see a resemblance that is not there, and that it is not lack of power and activity in the organ of Comparison which is responsible in such a case, but, rather, feebleness of the faculty of colour. With the denial of the relative powers of comparison and contrast, he is also implicitly denying Locke's judgement of the relative values of wit and judgement. He never makes the defence explicit, but the entire letter contains the unspoken assumption that wit is an activity of the intellect, not merely the emotions. The distinction is primarily important as showing that it was possible to take a serious view of the function of wit.

It would be pleasant to record that assigning intellect and emotion to specific places in the brain lessened the tangled wreaths of language into which most writers braid themselves when writing of abstract subjects, but the truth is that phrenologists more often than not seem to have been totally enmeshed by their attempts at communication. It was not long before they had arrived at what seemed to them the sensible conclusion that the organ of Wit had nothing whatsoever to do with what the man in the street called wit. It is a lamentable truth that almost all theoreticians about comedy, wit, and humour wind up holding views that a majority of people would fail totally to recognize as having anything to do with what they had always assumed those words meant. What is unusual about the phrenologists is that even within the bounds of their own specialized vocabulary they were unable to communicate.

In 1827, shortly after the appearance of Scott's article, a correspondent who identified himself only as 'X.T.P.H.' questioned the assumption that the organ of Wit was even incidentally related to 'Wit, in the common acceptation of the word' (IV, 369); Scott had asserted that the former was concerned with disparity, and Locke had said that the latter was the result of comparison. The disparate bases from which Mr. X.T.P.H. argues are shaky in the 'Inquiry Concerning an Organ for the Feeling of the Ludicrous, Distinct from That of Wit'; once they are accepted, however, Scott's view of function must be mistaken.

To begin with, it was manifestly mistaken that the organ of

Wit could be both intellectual faculty, whose office it was 'either to perceive objects external to the mind, to form conceptions of things, or to discover relations, not *necessarily* connected with any feeling whatever', and sentimental faculty, whose work was 'to give some species of feeling, without forming any idea either of perception, conception or relation' (IV, 368). If Nature, he asked, had assigned a specific organ for the primitive feelings of Self-esteem, Love of Approbation, Cautiousness, Benevolence, Veneration, Hope, etc., was it not reasonable to suppose that there should be a similar separate organ for 'the feeling of the ludicrous, which to all appearance is as much an original feeling as any of the other sentiments'? It was scarcely logical that wit should be 'a mongrel faculty, partaking both of intellect and of sentiment'. If its function is that of giving 'the feeling of the ludicrous, then unquestionably it is a sentiment'. But if discrimination is its function, 'then it ought to be classed with the intellectual faculties' (IV, 364–5).

X.T.P.H. quotes Locke on resemblance and difference as the final authority and concludes that Scott must be wrong about the nature of wit and guilty of ascribing an activity which is primarily comparative to an organ that is basically discriminative. Therefore, 'the phrenological faculty of Wit has just nothing at all to do with Wit, commonly so called' (IV, 370).

Further, the correspondent notices with considerable good sense, it is a matter of common observation that many persons with highly developed intellectual powers, including those of both comparison and discrimination, have 'little or nothing of the faculty of giving a ludicrous effect to the operation of these faculties'. Hence it seems clear that the source of the ludicrous cannot be in

the phrenological faculty of Wit, nor any other intellectual faculty. . . . We would, therefore, propose an amendment on Mr Scott's analysis of Humour. Instead of saying, the talent for it is produced by Secretiveness in combination with Wit, we would be disposed to say, the talent of Humour is produced by Secretiveness in combination with some faculty . . . the function of which is to give the feeling of the ludicrous . . . (IV, 372).

In other words, X.T.P.H. was right back with Spurzheim in thinking that the ludicrous was merely an emotion, quite unconnected with intellect, and with Locke in believing that wit was the result of comparison alone. There was no link between Wit and wit, and the only sensible thing to do was to rename the organ of Wit, despite the fact that it had originally been given its name because of its supposed connection with what the ordinary man thought the word meant. And where Scott had at least been able to entertain the idea that there was a connection between the celerity of mind implied in the older meaning of wit, and the laughable implied in the newer, X.T.P.H. denies totally the intellectual status of the ludicrous.

In 1830 Hewett Watson wrote resignedly that 'there is no other organ the real nature of whose function is so little understood, and concerning which so much difference of opinion has existed at different times, as that of Wit'. Nor could he, in his 'Inquiry into the Function of Wit', resist the opportunity to set straight the muddled thinking of every one else who had considered the matter. Gall, Spurzheim, Scott, and G. M. Schwartz of Stockholm are all summarized and dismissed curtly: 'Facts seem to contradict each of these opinions' (VI, 451).*

During the course of his career as phrenologist Watson regarded himself as unique in his scientific approach to a subject about which others were content to speculate irresponsibly. 'But expositions of science require a degree of precision in matters of fact, an exactness in definitions, and a substantial basis for inferences and reasonings . . .' (XI, 382). For Watson precision primarily meant an inspection of the phrenological development of the writers about whose works one was writing, and he was quite content to confine much of his literary examination to the poetry written by an amateur, 'a true-born son of Erin' (which, truthfully, hardly rises to mediocrity) because he was presumably able to make close observations and measurements of the young man's head. 'As scientific truth, not sublimity, is our present quest, the quality of the manifestations is of comparatively little import, and we shall therefore choose the most apposite illustrations in preference

---

* It is only fair to Watson to record that some eight years later he wrote anonymously of this article: 'He was perhaps more successful in pointing out the fallacies or failures of others, than in establishing any more accurate view' ('On the Opinions of Phrenologists Touching the Function of the Organ Called Wit', XI [October 1838], 386).

to the best compositions' (VI, 452). It is a statement calculated to raise critical hackles.

Scott, 'with some plausibility', had supposed the function of wit to be the perception of differences. However, 'Mr Scott's ideas of contrast are no longer tenable, inasmuch as the poet Moore, in whose mask Wit is but moderately developed, evinces a very considerable perception of difference' (VI, 451). By an opinion as simple and sweeping as this, Watson felt justified in rejecting some fifty pages of Scott's careful exposition.

Without wasting more time in preliminaries, he plunges into an announcement of his own position: 'In our opinion, the function of Wit is *intellectual* perception, not mere feeling; and, although many arguments of a metaphysical nature might be adduced in support of this opinion, it seems better not to consume space or time by combating shadows with shadows, however successfully it might be done, but to proceed at once to the more tangible logic of manifestation and development' (VI, 451–2).

What Watson had chiefly to offer was a considerable expansion of a point that he nowhere acknowledges had already been suggested by Scott, who had written that comparisons and contrasts can only be made between members of a group, that is between those which shared some common bond. Watson emphasizes that resemblances can be traced only between objects whose 'intrinsic' nature is the same. If the function of the organ of Wit is, as he suggests, to seek out that intrinsic linkage, then the function is very far indeed from being only the production of the ludicrous.

It would hence seem, that where Wit is large, comparisons of mere conditions are felt to be superficial, and that this organ would suggest comparisons where the resemblance extends beyond the temporary state; but if we are right in attributing the preceding manifestation to this organ, it must at once get a reprieve from its laughter-loving doom, and be permitted at times to put off its broad grins for the sober seriousness with which the said verses are written; and indeed we have long believed it as correct to convict the nightingale of being all song and no sleep, or the changeable physiognomy of April of being all smiles and no tears, as to accuse this ill-used organ of being all folly and no philosophy (VI, 453).

On these grounds Scott stands condemned of double error. First, he has confused wit with the organ of Wit, and second, he has been mistaken in thinking that the distinguishing quality of wit was contrast, and, worst of all, great breadth of contrast.

Puns, according to Watson, 'are observed to be sometimes connected with the organ of Wit: but, in this case, they are never limited to a mere play on the sound or equivalents of words, as often happens when they are the offspring of Language only. They are on the ideas attached to the words with or without a play on the sound' (VI, 454). Although it is difficult to imagine a pun without a play on the sound, we may notice that Watson has hit upon a point that eluded most of the nineteenth century, the distinction between the 'good' pun (which actually brings out an unexpected linkage of ideas) and the pun dependent upon purely fortuitous likeness of sound. In spite of his rough words about metaphysical writing, Watson is verging on a definition of wit that is not far off the metaphysical conceit.

Scott had suggested, quoting Beattie, that another source of wit was inappropriateness or incongruity of cause and effect. This, wrote Watson, is actually a function of the organ of Causality when the relations are merely between conditions or external phenomena; the disproportion becomes the function of wit only when the cause and effect are concerned with the 'nature and properties of things' (VI, 457).

The claim that Watson makes for wit is large; the only difficulty is that it no longer has much to do with the normal meaning of the word. It is hardly surprising when, in speaking of Sterne's classification of travellers in *A Sentimental Journey*, Watson claims that 'there is in these distinctions an admixture both of Philosophy and Wit, but certainly more of the former; and if our readers have gone along with our previous conclusions, they will scarcely hesitate to attribute both the one and the other to the organ bearing the cognomen of the latter' (VI, 459). To equate wit and philosophy is essentially to deny completely the connection between wit and the ludicrous.

One may wonder whether Watson's attitude does not owe its inception more to his lack of literary tact (and, perhaps, philosophical naïveté) than to a considered system of thought. For instance, he also observes of *A Sentimental Journey* that 'almost the whole tenor of this work, unlike that of most tourists, consists of disquisitions concerning the dispositions and inherent qualities of persons and things; for, instead of narrating who and what he saw, his attention seems to have been absorbed in speculations as to their conditions, dependences, nature, and qualities' (VI, 458). True, but most readers would have been less struck by the quality of Yorick's philosophical speculations than by the fun Sterne is having with them.

According to Watson's observations, in Sterne's 'mask Causality and Wit are predominating organs' (VI, 458). He is ignorant, he says, of the cerebral organization of Cowper, Rabelais, Butler, and Cervantes, 'but probably the organ of Wit would not be so largely developed in them, or in Swift, as in Sterne, Voltaire, and some others; though still by no means deficient in Butler . . .' He is led to doubt that it is a predominating organ in those authors 'because in other instances a very high endowment of any organ seems to give a tendency to the minutest discriminations and comparisons between its peculiar perceptions, while in these authors the similies are often palpable likenesses, and the contrasts drawn between things very unlike . . .' Then, in a flash of perception about his own powers as a reader, he recognizes the possibility that he had missed in writing of Sterne: that the authors may not be writing straightforwardly and that 'many of the apparently unnecessary distinctions and self-evident similitudes, may have been intended as burlesques, the key to which is now lost . . .' (VI, 460).

Some of Watson's judgements of other phrenologists and writers may be at least as revealing of his own mind as of theirs. 'In the bust of Dr Gall the organ is represented much less developed than in that of Dr Spurzheim; and the superiority of the latter in discriminating modes of manifestation and particular directions of the mental powers from the powers themselves, is familiar to all phrenologists.' Then, in one of his casual asides, he dismisses the very philosopher from whose writings most of the phrenologists had derived their arguments: 'Perhaps, too, we shall not err in adducing Locke as a negative instance of the faculty' (VI, 465).

Sheridan had 'enjoyed no slight reputation as a wit', but he was largely blind to 'attributes or inherent properties' (VI,

460). Comparison of his mask with that of other men not known for his type of wit shows that he had a moderate 'endowment of this organ'. Hence, if the individuals who have superior developments of the organ have 'a peculiar tendency to dwell on the essential properties of things, and, at the same time, in some of them an equal tendency to ridicule all fancy, philosophy, and reasoning, wherein there appears neglect or ignorance of these attributes', and if ludicrous wit in such men as Sheridan is found in conjunction with a deficient endowment of the organ, 'we shall be almost necessarily forced to the conclusion that perception of inherent properties does depend on the organ of wit . . .' (VI, 464).

Watson's article is in part phrenological in trying to determine the function of a particular part of the brain, but it is also what he calls 'metaphysical' or theoretical about the nature of wit and the ludicrous. It is not always easy to see why he clings to the label given the organ of Wit by Spurzheim, since it would seem simpler for him merely to suggest a different name to suit a different function than to differentiate between two totally disparate functions by the change of capitalization. The question is particularly puzzling because the essay is a complete renunciation of what Gall and Spurzheim had written on the matter. It is not quite enough to suggest that he had no idea of wit as ludicrous; perhaps it is simplest to conclude that the quality of his remarks about literature indicates that he was not totally at ease with it, or with other forms of the laughable, and that he greatly distrusted what he did not understand. It was a distrust that he shared with many of his contemporaries.

George Combe, who had been converted by Spurzheim's demonstrations and lectures in 1815, published the first edition of *A System of Phrenology* in 1819, a year before the founding of the Phrenological Society, but he continued expanding and revising the book until the fifth edition a quarter of a century later.[8] One of the subjects that was most expanded was his consideration of wit and humour, a large part of which was based upon Spurzheim, Scott, and Watson.

Combe's own examples and comments do not always inspire confidence in his ability to theorize about wit or laughter. He tells, for instance, the famous story of the notoriously rude

Louis XV, who noticed that Lord Stair's face was startlingly like his own. 'A remarkable likeness, upon my word!—My Lord, was your *mother* ever in France?' With the greatest of politeness and deference Stair replied, 'No, please your majesty, but my *father* was.' Combe says of the story: 'This also is admirably witty; but it does not excite laughter' (I, 491). One can only wonder what was required to make Combe laugh.

Like the other phrenologists, Combe assumes incongruity as the basis of wit, but to make his point he somewhat oversimplifies the positions of Spurzheim and Scott, suggesting that the former says that comparison 'takes cognizance not only of resemblances but also of differences. This view is opposed by Mr Scott, who attributes the perception of differences to the organ of Wit . . .' (II, 153). Actually, as we have seen, there was no real opposition between the views of the two men, only a difference in emphasis.

Combe quotes Scott at length, but his real indebtedness is obviously to Spurzheim; not the least of his agreement with Spurzheim is that he constantly assumes that there is some connection between the organ of Wit and the ludicrous. The section of his *System* which is primarily concerned with the matter is called 'Wit, or Mirthfulness'. It is true that he recognizes that laughter may spring from many other causes than wit. A person with a large organ of Acquisitiveness, for example, laughs when given a penny; one with a highly developed organ of Destruction laughs at the misfortunes of others, and so on. At last he states concisely his own view, 'that the organ [Wit] in question manifests the sentiment of the ludicrous, and that wit consists in any form of intellectual conception combined with this sentiment. . . . It appears to me that the ludicrous is merely *a mode of existence*, of which almost all natural objects are susceptible, but which is not the sole or necessary characteristic of any of them' (I, 501–2).

It is apparent here that Combe shares Spurzheim's view of wit as an emotion, even a generalized attitude, rather than a primarily intellectual process. 'I so far embrace Dr Spurzheim's views as to regard the sentiment of the ludicrous as the primitive function of the organ' (I, 503). This is not to say that he has discarded the theory of incongruity, for the emotion is not evoked until an object, person, or idea is measured against something else: 'there is no object in nature which in itself is essentially and necessarily ludicrous or absurd' (I, 502). The last word casually inserts the further assumption of superiority as another factor in the ludicrous.

Since there is nothing inherently witty or funny, according to Combe, it is not startling that there has been such confusion about the limits of the laughable. 'If no object whatever be in its own nature ludicrous, and if every mundane object may assume a ludicrous aspect as one of its modes of existence, it is clear that any definition, or even description of the ludicrous, as a specific entity, must be impossible' (I, 503).

Although one may feel that a sentiment incapable of definition does not get us very far in the consideration of wit and the ludicrous, Combe at least has loosened up the categories sufficiently to account for types of laughter that were avoided or clumsily handled by the other phrenologists. For example, when Wit predominates over Causality, the result is the farcical or the purely ludicrous, to the neglect of 'the intrinsic and of all the other philosophical quality of things' (I, 503). To say that a general disposition to laughter predominating over any close observation of cause-and-effect results in comedy or humour of an unthinking kind is at least as satisfactory as Watson's constant assertion that lower forms of laughter and wit are the result of insufficient comparison of their inherent natures. Furthermore, Combe's looseness of definition avoids the error into which both Watson and Locke fell, that of saying that wit deals only with comparisons, since comparison (as Combe notices) may degenerate into mere simile which can be beautiful or poetic without being in any way witty (I, 493).

Once we accept Combe's phrenological terms and translate them into more comprehensible language, he gives a good account both of ridicule and of the whole objection to wit dependent upon superiority. 'The sentiment of the ludicrous, acting in combination with Self-Esteem, produces ridicule. There is always an implied self-superiority in the individual who laughs at others. . . . such sallies are highly relished by individuals possessing the same combination with their authors' (I, 506).* Like Scott, he is here suggesting that not only is the

---

* One is reminded here of Watson's invocation of a different organ to explain a similar phenomenon, that of satire: 'the disgusts and fastidiousness

quality of mind of the reader or audience important in understanding the reaction to wit, but that there must be a kind of
likeness between the minds of the author and the reader. It is
this mysterious transmission of perception from one mind to
another that has always been the central problem of comedy
—and perhaps of all art. His suggestion is not profound, but it
is eminently sensible.

Combe is not to be swallowed whole as the final word of the
phrenologists on the subject of wit, but his attitudes are clearly
assumed as a kind of adjustment or balancing of the various
views postulated earlier by other phrenologists.

As has been suggested already, the phrenologists made no
revolutionary contributions to comic theory, but they served
to keep the subject alive for discussion and treated it with the
respect due to a fundamentally serious form of literature and
thought. For the twentieth century their views are important
because they are the assumptions of a group of intelligent,
well-educated men who mirrored the speculations of more
original thinkers. The necessity of reformulating the distinctions both indicates the importance of the subject to their
own times and provides us with a guide to the sensibility of the
nineteenth century on this debate.

No doubt many non-phrenologists shared De Quincey's
exasperation over definitions. 'What is wit?' he asks fret-
fully. 'We are told that it is the perception of resemblances;
whilst the perception of differences, we are requested to believe,
is reserved for another faculty. Very profound distinctions, no
doubt; but very senseless for all that.'[9]

---

of Ideality' ('Inquiry into the Function of Wit', *Phrenological Journal*,
VI, 451).

## CHAPTER V

# Sydney Smith, Leigh Hunt, and Thackeray

SYDNEY Smith's volume of *Elementary Sketches of Moral Philosophy* is the printed version of lectures that he delivered from 1804 until 1806, which hardly qualifies them as typically Victorian. The truth is that they were not generally known until their posthumous publication in 1850, after which they were widely read and quoted for a quarter of a century, so that their influence was much greater in mid-Victorian England than at the time of their delivery.

Probably much of their popularity was due to Smith's own reputation as a wit, a reputation that he constantly found an embarrassment during his clerical life and which was said to have kept him from being elevated to a bishopric. (One wonders whether his cautious approach to comedy in his two lectures 'On Wit and Humour' was the result of his awareness that a character as a wit was seldom the path to ecclesiastical preferment.) To Victorian critics the importance of the lectures was as a mine of quotations to lend substance to almost any theory of comedy. In them Smith seems to hesitate irresolutely before almost every pair of alternatives, then to attempt to seize them both.

The first lecture begins with a brief survey of seventeenth-century theory, then passes to Locke, who had made the 'first definition of wit worth noticing' (p. 118). The difficulty with Locke's formulation is that it is too comprehensive, for 'putting those ideas together with quickness and variety wherein can be found any resemblance or congruity' is a process that Smith recognizes may include both eloquence and poetry that are not even remotely risible (p. 119). Metaphor and symbolic thinking necessarily involve the illumination of previously unperceived linkages and relationships, and they are the foundation of poetry as much as of wit. Yet it is observable that the sublime and the beautiful which characterize poetry are not characteristic of wit. For Smith the problem becomes that of

F

finding aspects of the combination of ideas in wit that are not shared by poetry.

He mentions neither Imagination nor Fancy specifically, but the distinction between poetry and wit is constantly parallel to that between the two functions of mind. Wit, he tells us, can be deliberately cultivated, so is not unattainable, as are either beauty or 'just proportion'. Tongue in cheek, he declares solemnly that

I am so much of a contrary way of thinking, that I am convinced a man might sit down as systematically, and as successfully, to the study of wit, as he might to the study of mathematics: and I would answer for it, that, by giving up only six hours a day to being witty, he should come on prodigiously before midsummer, so that his friends should hardly know him again (p. 129).

Fancy, as the Romantics were fond of saying, was akin to mathematics in that both were involved with immutable, limited relationships, unlike those perceived by the Imagination.

The first aspect of wit that distinguishes it from poetry is surprise, which is no necessary constituent of poetry, where one may take pleasure in the establishment of an expected relationship. In wit surprise is so essential that no wit can bear repetition; 'the original electrical feeling produced by any piece of wit can never be renewed' (p. 122). Its importance is such that it is possible to produce a sensation much like that induced by wit, by the perception of surprising relationships in things that are otherwise totally divorced from wit; what results is, in Smith's fine phrase, 'the sensation of wit' (p. 124).

The second distinguishing aspect of wit is that it must not be mingled with ideas of the beautiful, sublime, angry, or pathetic, and that one must not reflect upon the utility of the relationships established in the bringing together of unlike ideas. Any such intrusive feelings will be antipathetic to wit, just as wit would be destructive of a consideration of the beautiful or the sublime. In other words, the relations between ideas must excite surprise, and surprise only (pp. 125–6).

Finally, wit is dependent upon a certain 'display of talent' to see the relations between facts; if it takes no intelligence to see the relation, there is no wit. Synthesizing his criteria, Smith says that 'whenever there is a superior act of intelligence in discovering a relation between ideas, which relation excites surprise and no other high emotion, the mind will have the feeling of wit' (p. 128).

At first glance Smith seems to be making exalted claims for wit, but that impression is lessened when one considers that the only result of 'a superior act of intelligence' is 'surprise and no other high emotion'.

The 'wit of words', puns, are in the same relation 'to words which wit is to ideas'. 'I have very little to say about puns; they are in very bad repute, and so they *ought* to be. The wit of language is so miserably inferior to the wit of ideas, that it is very deservedly driven out of good company' (p. 130). Either Smith is attempting to disclaim his own notorious addiction to punning, or he actually fails to see that puns may be a formidable weapon against the tyranny of language, and that they may serve to reveal real relationships of considerably greater importance than the mere chance likeness of sound shared by two words or phrases.

Irony he defines as 'the surprise excited by the discovery of that relation which exists between the apparent praise and the real blame' (p. 131); sarcasm 'consists in the obliquity of the invective' (p. 133). The consideration of such aspects of wit brings powerfully to Smith's mind the dangers of ridicule, which he momentarily appears to think of as synonymous with wit, and with it comes the fear of superiority in comedy that worried so many of his contemporaries. 'But learn from the earliest days to inure your principles against the perils of ridicule: you can no more exercise your reason, if you live in the constant dread of laughter, than you can enjoy your life, if you are in the constant terror of death' (p. 134). For him ridicule was no test of truth.

For Smith humour is much more akin to wit than one is used to considering it. Like wit, it normally takes its being from a form of basic incongruity rather than a feeling of superiority, and surprise 'is as essential to humour as it is to wit' (p. 137). There are, however, three real differences between humour and wit, concerned with manner, subject, and result.

Wit comes from the surprising comparison of apparently unlike ideas. In humour the 'cause is *incongruity*, or the con-

junction of objects and circumstances not usually combined,
—and the conjunction of which is either useless, or what in the
common estimation of men would be considered as rather
troublesome, and not to be desired' (p. 136). On the face of it,
the cause of humour is not very different from that of wit, save
that objects and circumstances are being combined, rather
than ideas. It becomes clear, however, that Smith believed (or
thought he believed) that the basis of wit was comparison, that
of humour contrast.

Wit and humour, though the first consists in discovering connection,
the latter in discovering incongruity, are closely and nearly related
to each other. The respective feelings, both depend upon surprise,
are both incompatible with serious and important ideas, and both
communicate the same sort of pleasure to the understanding
(p. 146).

The subject of wit, Smith asserted in the first lecture, is
always the relationships of ideas. Humour, however, is concerned with character, incident, fact, objects, externals: in
short (although he does not use the phrase) with the particular
rather than the general. The sensations of pleasure derived
from each are the same, although 'they may differ in degree,
for the incongruous observed of things living, is always more
striking than the incongruous observed in things inanimate;
but there *is* an incongruous not observable in character, which
produces the feeling of humour' (p. 140).

The rather rigid categories he employs sometimes trip
Smith. For instance, he includes the Irish 'bull' under humour
and says that it is the exact counterpart of wit, 'for as wit dis-
covers real relations that are not apparent, bulls admit apparent
relations that are not real' (p. 141). Because he is obliged to
say that all basic contrasts are humorous rather than witty, he
is forced into including in humour that which is really the
comedy of idea and of words, even though he perceives clearly
that wit and bulls operate in the same fashion.

The final distinction between wit and humour is in their
result, laughter, which 'is not so long and so loud in wit as it is
in humour'. This is probably because of the brevity of wit and
the cumulative effect of humour, 'to which, perhaps, may be

added, that wit excites more admiration than humour,—a feeling by no means favourable to laughter' (p. 145).

Smith gives no formal credence to the idea of sentimental comedy, yet at the same time he voices many of the objections to older definitions of comedy that gave rise to sentimental comedy.

The sense of the humorous is as incompatible with tenderness and respect as with compassion. No man would laugh to see a little child fall; and he would be shocked to see such an accident happen to an old man, or a woman, or to his father! . . . Whenever the man of humour meddles with these things ['our great and ardent hope of a world to come'], he is astonished to find, that in all the great feelings of their nature the mass of mankind always think and act aright;—that they are ready enough to laugh,—but that they are quite as ready to drive away with indignation and contempt, the light fool who comes with the feather of wit to crumble the bulwarks of truth, and to beat down the Temples of God! (pp. 138–9).

Smith's terminology is unlike that of, say, Carlyle, but his attitudes are not far different. Whatever his attitudes may have seemed at first, sentimentality and the disbelief in comedy as a method of intellectual investigation can scarcely go further.

In humour, as in wit, there is always the danger of feelings of superiority when one is laughing *at* another; 'at the same time, contempt accompanied by laughter, is always mitigated by laughter, which seems to diminish hatred, as perspiration diminishes heat' (p. 143). Smith seems in both lectures to have sallied forth bravely to establish the principle of incongruity as the underlying one in comedy, then to have assented wearily that perhaps after all it is really superiority that tells.

In the same fashion the close of the second lecture seems a complete volte-face from what has preceded. Where wit 'stands out boldly and emphatically', unrestrained by 'more serious qualities of mind', the probable tendency of both wit and humour is 'to corrupt the understanding and the heart' (p. 149). The independence of Smith's thinking has collapsed completely and he seems subserviently to be ending on the pious note of distrust of wit and humour that he apparently thought his audiences expected. He has become all things to all men; it is no wonder that his two lectures were so often mined and quoted by Victorian critics of totally unlike opinions.

The theorist of comedy is traditionally unsmiling at best, and probably even gloomy. Leigh Hunt was not an oversubtle critic, but he brought so his book on *Wit and Humour* the great advantage of a willingness to accept the pleasures of comedy and a belief that sunniness need not degenerate into chill reserve. Such an approach does not guarantee brilliance, but it is apt to preserve the critic from an excess of theory. In writing of Marvell's 'Description of Holland', he tells a story for other purposes that charmingly makes the point:

To enjoy it thoroughly, it is necessary perhaps that the reader should be capable, in some degree, of the like sort of jesting, or at least have animal spirits enough to run willing riot with the extravagance. Mr. Hazlitt, for defect of these, could see no kind of joke in it, notwithstanding his admiration of Marvel. He once began an argument with Charles Lamb and myself, to prove to us that we ought not to laugh at such things. Somebody meanwhile was reading the verses; and the only answer which they left us the power to make to our critical friend was by laughing immeasurably (pp. 237–8).

One more often longs for the gaiety and spontaneity of Lamb and Hunt in comic theoreticians than for the moderation of Hazlitt.

It was perhaps his own personality, rather than a carefully considered critical position, that led Hunt towards a redefinition of wit and humour that would admit that there were pleasures derivative from the intellect that were neither superior, malicious, nor condescending. The basis of both wit and humour seemed to him to be incongruity. Laughter at wit is the result of 'a sudden and agreeable perception of the incongruous' (p. 8), and what separates wit from humour is not attitude but the nature of the subject-matter. Humour 'deals in incongruities of character and circumstances, as Wit does in those of arbitrary ideas' (p. 12).

Hunt is anticipating the point that lies behind Schopenhauer's theory of comedy as paradox, when he stresses that the result of the best comedy is reconciliation, not disparity. The 'sudden and agreeable perception' derives its pleasure from a 'jar' that is then resolved. 'It is in these reconcilements of jars, these creations and re-adjustments of disparities, that the delightful faculty of the wit and humorist is made manifest' (p. 8). Suddenly one feels the bracing wind of intellect, the recognition that reason may have its pleasures of which the heart knows nothing. 'Happy', 'delightful', 'lively', 'agreeable', the adjectives keep recurring in reference to wit and the mind. This is not to suggest at all that Hunt was lacking in appreciation of the pleasures of the humour of character, only that he recognized that comedy at its best comes from the whole of man, that the emotions and the intellect are not necessarily in conflict. Without probing very deeply into theory, Hunt recognizes instinctively what many critics of his time were at pains to deny.

Hunt considers both humour and wit, but it is to the latter that he obviously gives his allegiance: a wit that owes its being to incongruity, *'the Arbitrary Juxtaposition of Dissimilar Ideas, for some lively purpose of Assimilation or Contrast, generally of both'* (p. 9). Superiority has no place in the 'occasions of pure mirth and fancy', when 'we only feel superior to the pleasant defiance which is given to our wit and comprehension; we triumph, not insolently but congenially; not to anyone's disadvantage, but simply to our own joy and reassurance' (p. 7). There is a slight touch of Lewis Carroll about a situation in which triumph is congenial, everyone wins, and no one loses, but the process of his thought and the reasons behind it seem fairly clear. He is taking contemporary terminology and attempting to give it new currency by a definition to bridge the two theories of superiority and incongruity; or, to put the matter in another way, he is allowing the theory of superiority to stand at the very time that he is busy redefining superiority to mean incongruity. 'Two ideas are as necessary to Wit, as couples are to marriages,' and they must both remain separate and become one (perhaps the notion was easier to comprehend in an age when the doctrine of the Trinity was commonly accepted). It is this dual conception that lies constantly behind wit. 'The two-fold impression is not in every case equally distinct. You may have to substantiate it, critically; it may be discerned only on reflection; but discernible it is always' (pp. 10–11).

There is more critical wisdom in Hunt's asides than in his formal expositions and definitions. Probably in emulation of Barrow's minutely dissected forms of facetiousness, Hunt lists fourteen principal forms of wit, but there is little in the list to admire but ingenuity. His writing comes to sudden life when he is considering the authors from whose works he draws the examples of his theory. Chaucer is 'entertaining, profound, and good-natured', he says, but the last of these qualities may 'be thought a drawback by some' (p. 75). 'Shakespeare had as great a comic genius as tragic; and everybody would think so, were it possible for comedy to impress the mind as tragedy does' (p. 122). It is 'a remarkable proof' of the geniality of his jesting 'that even its abundance of ideas does not spoil it' (p. 124).

Although Samuel Butler had 'little humour', he was 'the wittiest of English poets, and at the same time he is one of the most learned, and what is more, one of the wisest'. In *Hudibras* the 'wit is pure and incessant; the learning is quaint and out-of-the-way as the subject' (pp. 242–4). If Hunt were 'requested to name the book of all others, which combined Wit and Humour under their highest appearance of levity with the profoundest wisdom, it would be *Tristram Shandy*' (p. 72). However platitudinous the idea seems to us, there were few Victorians who could see that risibility was not by its very nature incompatible with seriousness of idea or purpose.

*Wit and Humour* is in large part pastiche, presumably put together for quick sales; it is easy to see why Hunt was severely taken to task by the critics. It is an ill-organized book, and the proceeding theory seldom seems to be closely connected to the illustrating quotations. One reviewer in *Fraser's* said that the examples were 'miserable failures'. They were 'ushered forth with all the dignity of italics—which, indeed, is the only humorous thing about them'. However, as the *Dublin University Magazine* reviewer wrote, to exact 'scientific precision in criticism would be to require impossibilities. Mr. Hunt has done much better in giving us an exceedingly pleasant book—likely to add very much to the best and purest sources of enjoyment.'[1] Hunt did better than that: he produced one of the few pieces of mid-Victorian criticism of comedy that is remarkably free of cant.

Eight years later Hunt published his other major consideration of the subject, a short essay called 'On the Combination
of Grave and Gay'. As the title indicates, this is an attempt
to show that comedy is not incompatible with basic seriousness. Hunt does not assert that comedy itself is serious, as one
might expect from the implicit premises of *Wit and Humour*,
where earnestness, rather than seriousness, appears to be the
logical antithesis of comedy. In this essay he simply tries to
show that both gravity and gaiety are necessary components
of the best literature.

The combined faculty of serious and comic perception in
a writer should not surprise us, Hunt argues, since all men
ideally have both; anyone who is deficient in either is 'imper-
fectly organized, and no right average human creature' (p.
560). The reader, too, is gratified when the comic author
shows his power of being both 'serious and tender'. Obviously,
one's admiration is 'doubled by the sight of the double gift'.

To the amusement which is given our brains, is added the approbation of the heart. What might have seemed nothing but levity, is
found accompanied with the best kind of gravity. The man whom
we might have feared as a satirist, we think we might count upon
as a friend (p. 559).

It is narrow-minded to think that 'because a man is gay, he
cannot be grave; or that because he is grave, gaiety can never
become him'. Such an opinion, says Hunt, proceeds from the
'dulness of those who hold it, and from their inability to put
two ideas together'. Pascal, Saint Francis of Sales, Thomas
More, Luther, and Socrates are good examples of the union of
wit, dignity, and reverence (p. 561). The highest form of
literature is that which unites comedy and seriousness. Shakespeare, for example, could write as Milton did, he could think
with equal seriousness and express himself with a Miltonic
nobility, but Milton, because he lacked humour, 'could not
write like Shakspeare' (p. 560).

In the best of contemporary literature gravity acts as a
restraint to wit; 'the Dickenses, Jerrolds, and Thackerays' are
unusual in

the vein of tenderness which forms so beautiful an undercurrent
to their satire; and for that love of the general good, and that

freedom from personality for its own sake, which has exalted the
character of satire itself, and shown how it can be rendered a true
instrument of reformation (p. 563).

It was not sentimental comedy, however, that needed support,
and one imagines that the distrust of laughter attendant upon
it was not much to Hunt's taste in any case. Instead, he devotes
the largest part of the essay to the less popular assertion of the
necessity of laughter and gaiety. Christ Himself, he reminds us,
sat among the wine-bibbers at the wedding feast, 'and cheerfulness, nay mirth, is not easily to be supposed to have been
wanting' (p. 565).

Hunt was not specifically advancing the cause of intellectual
comedy, but he was certainly preparing the ground for its
reacceptance. His is not an important essay except that it is
a sensible statement, standing firmly on middle ground, denying the self-sufficiency of either extreme attitude towards
comedy. On the one hand, pure wit is inadequate, on the other,
sentiment without laughter is a diminution of life and art.

It would be unfair to Thackeray to judge him as critic from
the two major pieces of comic theory that he wrote. *English
Humourists of the Eighteenth Century* is a collection of six lectures
he delivered first in London in 1851. A year later he spoke on
'Charity and Humour' in New York. The longer series of
lectures was undertaken primarily as a means of making money
between novels, the single one on behalf of a charity when he
was lecturing in America (although he thriftily delivered it on
several later, unconnected occasions). Both were intended for
large audiences, presumably of limited enthusiasm for matters
critical, and it is not surprising that there are repetitions of
phrases and ideas in lectures separated by so little time. It
would be unjust, too, to suggest that the lectures, however
much alike they are, are totally representative of his views,
or that he was incapable of more analytical reasoning than is
displayed in either. They are, however, disturbingly short on
the consideration of humour apparently promised by their
titles, although one does get a tolerably accurate picture of his
formal views on comedy by piecing the hints together.

Presumably because he was speaking to audiences more

interested in entertainment than theory, more intent on hear-
ing a live novelist than on speculating about comedy, Thackeray introduced *English Humourists* by announcing that he
intended to speak 'of the men and of their lives, rather than
of their books'. The latter were to be dealt with 'only in as far
as they seem to illustrate the character of their writers' (pp.
3, 146). It did not misrepresent his opinions, however, for him
to concentrate on biography, since he took a sentimental view
of humour, and that view, as we have seen, is partly dependent
upon a belief that humour is the attempt to make sympathetic
contact with other characters. Thackeray took the theory a
step further and assumed a Ruskinian kind of identity between
the work of art and the personality and moral character of the
artist. It is a typically Victorian assumption, and a two-edged
one at that: if one knows the biography of a writer, it is possible to judge the quality of his work without reading it, since
a noble work of art can scarcely proceed from an ignoble mind.
On the other hand, if one reads the work, it is quite possible
to postulate the moral nature of its author without further
knowledge.

Such assumptions make the task of critic and biographer
easier, but they do not necessarily inspire confidence. Thus,
most modern readers would feel that Thackeray seriously
underrated Swift and Sterne because he was repelled by their
lives and personalities. However, he loved Steele's works, so
it was permissible to invent biographical fact to explain the
quality of his writing. 'I have no sort of authority for the state-
ments here made of Steele's early life,' he wrote; 'but if the
child is the father of the man . . . Dick Steele the schoolboy
must have been one of the most generous, good-for-nothing,
amiable little creatures . . . in Great Britain' (p. 100). As
Charles Whibley said of the series of lectures, Thackeray
'refused to recognise the tyranny of facts'.[2]

For Thackeray the comic writer is 'the week-day preacher',
who arouses scorn for lies, pretension, and impostures, while
he inspires 'tenderness for the weak, the poor, the oppressed,
the unhappy'. As it is the business of the humourist 'to mark
other people's lives and peculiarities', so 'we moralise upon
*his* life when he has gone—and yesterday's preacher becomes
the text for to-day's sermon' (p. 4).

Although the point of view of the lectures is that of the biographer (and good story-teller), Thackeray's obvious love is for sentimental comedy and therefore the sentimental humorists. When he finds a writer to his taste, he is full of ebullience, although it would be hard for anyone who has not read the lectures to imagine that he could manage great enthusiasm for Goldsmith as a humourist without ever mentioning that he wrote *She Stoops to Conquer*. When he is put off by either the character or the works of an author, what he has to say is poor indeed. It surely displays a total misunderstanding of Swift to find in 'A Modest Proposal' an exposure of 'the unreasonableness of loving and having children' (p. 30).

Distorted echoes of Lamb resound in Thackeray's consideration of Congreve; he was an observer 'to whom the world seems to have no morals at all, and whose ghastly doctrine seems to be that we should eat, drink, and be merry when we can' (p. 68). His reputation was won by a 'merry and shameless Comic Muse . . . a disreputable, daring, laughing, painted French baggage' (pp. 54–5). The famous description of Restoration comedy, endowed with all the attributes of Nell Gwynn, is one of Thackeray's elaborate set-pieces, full of the strings of nouns and adjectives with which he habitually attempted to give life to the past. 'She was kind and popular enough, that daring Comedy . . .' It was on moral grounds, not artistic, that Thackeray disapproved of both Nell and Congreve's plays. His comic muse was

gay and generous, kind, frank as such people can afford to be! and the men who lived with her and laughed with her, took her pay and drank her wine, turned out when the Puritans hooted her, to fight and defend her. But the jade was indefensible, and it is pretty certain her servants knew it (p. 55).

This kind of characterization has more place in a novel than in criticism; its importance is that it had sufficient validity to Thackeray for him to use it again (and one can only wonder whether it loitered in Meredith's mind when he characterized the Comic Muse in quite different terms in *The Egoist* and in his *Essay on Comedy*).

To Thackeray comedy was tolerable only when it warmed the heart of both writer and audience. Fielding's 'moral sense was blunted by his life', which is proved by his 'evident liking and admiration for Mr. [Tom] Jones'. It was absurd, he said, to create 'a hero with a flawed reputation; a hero spunging for a guinea; a hero who can't pay his landlady, and is obliged to let his honour out to hire' (p. 215). In spite of such failings Fielding's

wit is wonderfully wise and detective; it flashes upon a rogue and lightens up a rascal like a policeman's lantern. He is one of the manliest and kindliest of human beings: in the midst of all his imperfections, he respects female innocence and infantine tenderness as you would suppose such a great-hearted, courageous soul would respect and care for them. He could not be so brave, generous, truth-telling as he is, were he not infinitely merciful, pitiful, and tender (p. 211).

Repeatedly the same formula crops up in the lectures. The writer is credited with wit, but almost immediately Thackeray rushes on to what is important, the warmth of his heart.

If the lectures are not very valuable as theory, they are at least good litmus paper to show the quality of what Thackeray thought his audiences would react to. Since that quality appealed to Thackeray himself, it indicates how much at one he was with the popular Victorian formulations of humour. *English Humourists* has, understandably, not received much attention from critics of Thackeray's novels, and when it is mentioned it is often dismissed with a reference to his idiosyncratic definition of humour.[3] What is perhaps more to the point is that his definition owes its being to his casual acceptance of the popular meaning of the term; the lectures might have been far more interesting if he had only been a bit more idiosyncratic, had he bothered to make a definition himself, instead of using tired, outworn formulas.

Thackeray's attitudes towards comedy which lie behind the *English Humourists* are made totally explicit in his lecture on 'Charity and Humour', in which he takes the opportunity of speaking to a philanthropic audience in New York to show that charity and humour have the same purpose. Once more, it is necessary to be careful about assigning too much weight to the lecture, since it is said to have been written in a single day in preparation for lecturing at the Church of the Messiah for the

benefit of a poor-relief society, to an audience of 1,500.[4] However, the very ease with which it was dictated may have come
from the fact that Thackeray was making overt all the assumptions about humour that had been accepted but unstated in
the longer series of lectures.

In the beginning of the lecture he reverts to the phrase he had
used in *English Humourists* and calls the humourous writers
'our gay and kind week-day preachers', asking whether they
have not been active in the cause that had drawn the audience
together that night: 'the cause of love and charity, the cause
of the poor, the weak, and the unhappy; the sweet mission of
love and tenderness, and peace and goodwill towards men'?
(p. 268). He cites Addison, Steele, Fielding, Goldsmith, Hood,
and Dickens as those who confer benefit by their sermons, and
with what we can only imagine as a sigh of relief, he neglects
the recalcitrant Swift and Sterne and Congreve, who were
clearly difficult to fit into the pulpit of his making.

Humour is 'wit and love . . . the best humour is that which
contains most humanity . . .' (p. 270). There is 'no such provocative as humour' of tears. 'It is an irresistible sympathiser;
it surprises you into compassion: you are laughing and disarmed,
and suddenly forced into tears' (p. 279).

Humour! humour is the mistress of tears; she knows the way to the
*fons lachrymarum*, strikes in dry and rugged places with her enchant-
ing wand, and bids the fountain gush and sparkle. She has refreshed
myriads more from her natural springs than ever tragedy has
watered from her pompous old urn (p. 280).

Thackeray credits Steele with the beginnings of sentimental
comedy; he 'stepped off the high-heeled cothurnus, and came
down into common life'. He rescued comedy 'from behind the
fine lady's alcove', and at his touch adultery ceased to be a
tolerable subject for mirth.

That miserable rouged, tawdry, sparkling, hollow-hearted comedy
of the Restoration fled before him, and, like the wicked spirit in the
fairy-books, shrank, as Steele let the daylight in, and shrieked,
and shuddered, and vanished. The stage of humourists has been
common life ever since Steele's and Addison's time; the joys and
griefs, the aversions and sympathies, the laughter and tears of
nature (p. 277).

So much for Congreve, so much for Nell and the Restoration. What, one may ask, is the value of a theory of comedy that excludes Congreve? Or Sterne? Or Swift? Truly, it is puzzling to wonder what has become of laughter and of intelligence, and also—more puzzling still—what has become of Becky and Lord Steyne? Or of the amused attitudes towards Amelia and Dobbin that gleam through Thackeray's fondling of them?

There are indeed moments when one must rejoice that the creative natures of artists need not be bounded by their own strictures and criticism. As a novelist Thackeray can be maddeningly sentimental himself, but that is only one of his voices. It is a shame that he chose to neglect all others when he came to write about comedy. From these lectures it would be impossible to guess that he was capable of fine, astringent irony and a cool wit in his own novels. No doubt the composition of the audience to whom he was speaking was in part responsible for the tone of his lectures. If so, they got what they deserved.

'Charity and Humour' concludes with a famous tribute to the genius of Dickens. It is often quoted for its geniality, its generosity, its recognition of the greatness of a fellow artist. All this is true, but it might equally be quoted for its emetic quality. The tribute shows better than any comment why it was necessary, for the health of literature, that a little intellect should leaven what had been passing for comedy:

I may quarrel with Mr. Dickens's art a thousand and a thousand times; I delight and wonder at his genius; I recognise in it—I speak with awe and reverence—a commission from that Divine Beneficence, whose blessed task we know it will one day be to wipe every tear from every eye. Thankfully I take my share of the feast of love and kindness which this gentle, and generous, and charitable soul has contributed to the happiness of the world. I take and enjoy my share, and say a Benediction for the meal (p. 286).

As criticism, *English Humourists* and 'Charity and Humour' show only how enthralled Thackeray could be by popular cliché; as unintentional example it is superb.

## CHAPTER VI

# George Eliot, Leslie Stephen, and George Meredith

O NE of the difficulties in reading a large group of writings like those of the nineteenth century on comedy is that the whole vocabulary becomes tediously familiar. Some of the repetition of words and ideas is undoubtedly plagiarism in the final analysis: the vague tickle of a phrase may drive one to locate the source from which the echo emanates, only to find that phrases, sentences, even paragraphs have been shamelessly lifted. Occasionally they have been taken without alteration, more often they are artistically rearranged. A topic that has been analysed and argued over for centuries is naturally going to attract repetition of ideas to match that of diction. It is like a breath of fresh air to turn to 'German Wit: Heinrich Heine', the much too brief analysis of wit and humour by George Eliot. The essay is a beautiful demonstration of the fact that originality can walk hand in hand with erudition and complete knowledge of what others have thought on the same subject. Never is there any doubt about George Eliot's background and learning, but equally one is aware from moment to moment that it is her mind, not that of others, that is giving shape to the essay. Heritage is totally distinct from echo.

George Eliot may well be the most intellectual of English novelists, but the comedy of her own works is more often that of humour than of wit. Mrs. Poyser is a fair example of George Eliot's vein of laughter. In 1856, when she wrote 'German Wit', Mrs. Poyser still lay in the future, but one might expect that the talent capable of producing such characters would have a distinct bias in favour of humour over wit. This is not the case.

The essay itself is laid out with an introductory theoretical section on wit and humour, then a consideration (as much biographical as critical) of Heine. Without specifically alluding to the almost complete dominance of sentimental humour, George Eliot sets out to destroy the idea that there is anything in humour that necessarily demands sympathy; indeed, as she points out, it may be cruel and savage. It is, to be sure, more poetic than wit, but that is because it is 'of earlier growth', because it comes from a time when the intellectual faculties of the human race were underdeveloped. 'Humour draws its materials from situations and characteristics', which are more rudimentary than the 'unexpected and complex relations' on which wit seizes (p. 218). Schoolboys may joke, but they are not capable of comedy (p. 217).

In the boyhood of the intellect of the race, humour will be dominant, and it 'may co-exist with a great deal of barbarism, as we see in the Middle Ages'. But this kind of humour springs 'not from sympathy, but more probably from triumphant egoism or intolerance'. In other words, humour is to be accounted for quite as much as wit by the theory of superiority. Practical jokes, for example, may have a high degree of humour,

but no sympathetic nature can enjoy them. Strange as the genealogy may seem, the original parentage of that wonderful and delicious mixture of fun, fancy, philosophy, and feeling which constitutes modern humour, was probably the cruel mockery of a savage at the writhings of a suffering enemy . . .

The reason that most critics have been confused about the nature of humour is that those who are most eloquent about it have concentrated 'almost exclusively on its higher forms', neglecting the great body of humour. To define it as 'the *sympathetic* presentation of incongruous elements in human nature and life' is to dwell upon an unrepresentative section of humour (p. 219). As so often in the writings of George Eliot, one constantly feels that she is stripping her thinking of the accretive baggage of the restrictive formulations of others.

'Wit is more nearly allied to the ratiocinative intellect' (p. 218), which means that cultivated men can have no community with the vulgar in their jocularity. Wit 'demands a ripe and strong mental development' (p. 217), and it detects unsuspected analogies.

Every one who has had the opportunity of making the comparison
G

will remember that the effect produced on him by some witticisms is closely akin to the effect produced on him by subtle reasoning which lays open a fallacy or absurdity . . .

In its highest reaches wit deals not only with words but 'with the essential qualities of things'. Only its ingenuity, condensation, and quickness distinguish the highest wit from reasoning; it is *reasoning raised to a higher power* (p. 218).

With her usual good sense, George Eliot recognizes that wit and humour constantly overlap and blend, and that distinctions between them necessarily falsify in part. Rarely does either of them occur without some flavour of the other, and in the greatest of comic writers such as Shakespeare and Molière, they occur united at their highest pitch. In one of the few platitudes of the essay, she says that this union is a happy conjunction, 'for wit is apt to be cold, and thin-lipped, and Mephistophelean in men who have no relish for humour', while 'broad-faced, rollicking humour needs the refining influence of wit'.

All fine writing, she continues, contains at least some wit to give brightness and transparency, and it is particularly necessary in humorous writing, for humour is essentially without organization, has no limit but its own exuberance, and becomes tiresome and preposterous without the check of wit, 'which is the enemy of all monotony, of all lengthiness, of all exaggeration' (p. 220).

The introduction to Heine concludes with a long and very funny contrast of typically humourless wit in the French and the archetypal unrelieved humour of the German. Once more George Eliot's preference is surprising, for the woman we often think of as the mid-century's most important advocate and popularizer of German literature[1] clearly has little use for that nation's sense of humour, which generally has 'no sense of measure, no instinctive tact; it is either floundering and clumsy . . . or laborious and interminable as a Lapland day, in which one loses all hope that the stars and quiet will ever come'. Even Jean Paul is always unendurable to some readers and 'frequently tiresome to all'. German comedy, like German sentences, has no structural reason ever to conclude, and the ending seems 'an arrangement of Providence rather than the author' (p. 221). Only Lessing among the Germans has any claim to wit (p. 222).

No one reveres and treasures the products of the German mind more than we do. To say that that mind is not fertile in wit, is only like saying that excellent wheat land is not rich pasture; to say that we do not enjoy German facetiousness, is no more than to say, that though the horse is the finest of quadrupeds, we do not like him to lay his hoof playfully on our shoulder (p. 223).

One is constantly aware in reading this fine essay that the introductory, theoretical section is but slightly related to the consideration of Heine that follows. It seems probable that the reason why George Eliot included the generalized treatment of wit and humour (the latter is not even mentioned in the title of her essay) is that she was restless at the thoughtless repetition of the superiority of a castrated and sentimental humour over the product of the ratiocinative intellect. She quotes Goethe as saying that nothing is more indicative of men's characters than what they find laughable. 'The truth of this observation would perhaps have been more apparent', she comments wryly, 'if he had said *culture* instead of character' (p. 217). What she wrote was a blow on behalf of culture against sentimentality. One perhaps may be forgiven for thinking that it was a shame it took at least another twenty years for most of her contemporaries to heed her advice.

Although he wrote several articles concerned with the nature of comedy, Leslie Stephen's main consideration of the subject is the *Cornhill* article of March 1876 that he somewhat misleadingly called 'Humour'. The title makes the reader expect still another of the Victorian essays on the warm, sympathetic comforts of humorous writing; instead, what we find is a brilliant, quirky sapping of the very foundations of the conceptions supporting sentimental humour. Rather than attempt to change popular ideas of comedy by extolling the virtues of intellectual wit, Stephen tears headlong into the preconceptions shared by most of the Victorian humorists.

The essay was probably a by-product of Stephen's reading and research for his two-volume *History of English Thought in the Eighteenth Century*, which was published the same year and which treats comic theory in passing. Although the comparison is not made directly, the burden of the essay is the difference between the virility of the comedy of the eighteenth century and the feebleness of the sentimentality that had overtaken humour in his own day.

One of the difficulties of the ironical tone that Stephen adopted for this essay is that it is frequently hard to follow his quick and unannounced changes of persona as he alternates between his own views about the nature of humour and his ironic assumption of those held by the contemporaries whom he was attacking. It is intended for close scrutiny only, and some of his *Cornhill* readers must have put down the magazine in bafflement. It is worth the difficulty, however, for it is an urbanely savage performance not unworthy of comparison to the irony of his greatly admired Swift.

'If people were to be taken at their own valuation,' he begins mildly, 'logical acumen and a keen perception of the humorous would be the two most universal qualities in the world'. Then, one by one, he dismisses the Scots, French, Germans, Irish, and Americans, leaving only 'the true kindly genial flavour of the English article'. The rest of the essay is devoted to showing that nothing could be further from a true humour than what passes under that name in England. A writer who is looking for a successful career may be dull, or bombastic, or sentimental, or flimsy, or even muddled; what he must avoid at all costs is humour. 'We enjoy Shakspeare's humour; but he has been dead a long time, . . . we are fond of Charles Lamb, but Lamb's writings were caviare to the public whilst he lived, . . . we read Mark Twain and Artemus Ward, and perhaps to a calm observer that is the most conclusive proof of all that we have very little notion of what true humour means' (pp. 318–19).

Carlyle, Stephen thought, was largely responsible for the great belief in the necessity of having a sense of what passes for humour. 'His humour is so genuine and keen and his personality so vigorous that he has fairly bullied us into accepting this view' (p. 319). Yet those qualities most antithetic to true humour—priggishness, platitude, belief in cliques—have never flourished more vigorously.

Stephen accepts without question that humour and wit are

both the result of contrast and incongruity, and that it is not necessary to define them much further than that, or, indeed, possible to do so. Humour is seldom allied with philosophy, which can make definitions. 'The thinker loves symmetry, the humorist hates it; and therefore the two classes are radically opposed; which, one may suppose, is one argument against the merits of humour' (pp. 319–20). Wit comes of the 'electric sparks that flash out when some circuit of reasoning is unexpectedly completed', humour 'implies the love of emotional contrasts' (pp. 320, 322). Further distinction is useless.

What Stephen is asserting is the total connection between wit and the best of humour. Intellect and emotion become, in his thinking, differing subjects of comedy not methods of approaching it. No longer are they unlike or antithetical; they are both manifestations of a common manner of thought, that of comedy. Comedy appeals to incongruity or disparity between aspects of what is being considered, not to the consanguinity of feeling between the characters of comedy and their author or audience. Sentiments and emotions may be the stuff of humour, but the final perception of their meaning is intellectual not sentimental. There is certainly an appeal to superiority when the incongruity is between the ideal and the actual, but the reality of comedy is always the awareness of incongruity. In short, comedy may include feelings of superiority, but it cannot exist without the perception of incongruity.

With wicked accuracy Stephen parodies contemporary descriptions of the humorist,

the man who laughs through tears. In the fabric of his emotions the warp of melancholy is crossed by the woof of cheerfulness. (I am not acquainted with warps and woofs in common life, but they are mentioned in Gray's Ode, and seem to be specially intended for literary use.) His writing is a play of cross lights, sunshine, and shadow dexterously intermingled or completely fused into a contradictory unity. . . . You cannot tell whether a cathedral will most affect him with an awe of the infinite or an exhibition of tumblers at a pantomime. He will even laugh at the Social Science Association.

And there is nothing the humorist hates more than a scientific truth, since he cannot shape it curiously to fit his own mind. It is idiosyncrasy, not truth, that the humorist seeks in sentimental comedy.

As sentimental humour seeks idiosyncrasy in others, it becomes increasingly tolerant, even proud of finding oddity in the character of the humorist himself. However much contemporary ideas of humour proclaim sympathy with others, they are fundamentally based on egotism and selfishness: ' . . . above all, the humorist must also be an egotist. The oddities of his own character give him the utmost delight. He cherishes his whims and the arbitrary twists of his moral nature, for fear that he should lapse into straightforward simplicity of sentiment' (p. 320). It is hard to refrain from speculating on whether Stephen's friend Meredith had this passage in mind when he named his most famous novel.

In the essay Stephen is not really attacking humour, only the mode of redefinition that had removed it from its primary meaning, that had taken away all associations of vigour and risibility. Humour (and here Stephen apparently means all comedy) is not a simple way of warming the heart; it must have a double edge that will kill off false enthusiasm as quickly as it will check undeserved contempt. Love and sympathy, however one may approve of them, are simply not necessary components of humour. To the Victorians a gentle smile, a delighted chuckle were all the laughter that humour allowed, but that was because they were finally not taking a serious view of the world. 'The humorist loves the kind of virtuous character who can be made into a pretty plaything,' so long as the character is only 'rather ridiculous', but he stops caring 'for them when they insist upon taking things seriously' (p. 323).

The devotee of sentimental humour will cry 'over the semi-idiotic organist in *Martin Chuzzlewit*, or any sentimental moralist who . . . curses the very name of Malthus'. But when humour becomes allied with vigorous principle attempting to right wrong, 'then your humorist cannot find variations enough upon the old cry of hypocrite, humbug, impostor' (p. 323). The humorist loves Dickens for the quality that offends true lovers of comedy: his ability to drop humour 'and become purely and simply maudlin at a moment's notice' (p. 325).

Quite obviously, Stephen resented most of Dickens, but he probably felt that much of his essay would be forgotten in indignation if he were to concentrate his attack upon the best-loved of Victorian novelists. Instead, he turns to another comic novelist, one who seemed to him as removed from the real world as Dickens. 'I never . . . knew a person thoroughly deaf to humour who did not worship Miss Austen' (p. 324). She is never improper, and her books would be thoroughly appropriate as presents to a clergyman's daughter, but equally there is never a flash of satire in them. She inhabits her peaceful world in comfort, never hinting that squires and parsons

are not an essential part of the order of things; if she touches upon poverty, the only reflection suggested is one of gentle scorn for people who can't keep a butler themselves or take tea with people who do so. When the amiable Fanny Price in *Mansfield Park* finds that her mother has to eat cold mutton and mend the children's clothes, her only thought is to return to her rich uncle (p. 325).

What Stephen is asking for is considerably more than true humour; he is demanding a total social involvement in the novelist, rather than the insipid 'creed of the gentler variety of humorist', which seems to be the moral of Dickens's *Christmas Carol*: 'Let us all drink plenty of milk-punch and forget the laws of Political Economy' (pp. 326, 325). It is true that he seems to be moving some distance from comedy, that much of what he thinks comedy should be is very akin to social satire, and that by modern standards he totally misunderstands both Jane Austen and Dickens. All the same, the importance of the essay is that he is demanding that the comic be taken seriously, asserting that it is far more than a plaything for idle hours. Whatever one may say of contemporary literature, he says, 'nobody will ever call it manly. The general want of vigour is perhaps after all at the bottom of the deficiency in good hearty reckless humour . . .' (p. 326).

Stephen's view of literature is a large one; just as wit and humour are part of the same mode of thought, so that mode, comedy, is indivisible from the rest of literature. Probably it would not be unfair to him to work backwards and to say that since literature is to him such a serious matter, then all responsible forms of it, including comedy, must partake of that seriousness. He seems to have come a long way from the sentimental view of humour.

George Meredith's style was seldom his best friend, except when its complexity served to hide the simplicity of thought that it

clothed. *An Essay on Comedy*, to give it its most familiar name,[2]
has never settled comfortably into the canon of either works by
Meredith or works on comedy. Partly, one suspects, the baffled
incomprehension that so often greets a reading of this essay is
due to its lack of organization and to the tortuous prose in
which it is couched. (The fact that the prose is somewhat
simpler than that of many of his novels is irrelevant.) V. S.
Pritchett has pointed out that, as lectures, much of the essay
may have worked in performance, 'but one is never quite sure
(outside of one or two eloquent passages), what he is saying
half the time'.[3] The reaction is no doubt more honest than
some others that have been recorded, but it is probably far
from untypical. Most of the books on Meredith simply ignore
the essay except to say that it began as a pair of lectures in 1877.

But the difficulty of Meredith's prose constantly leads readers
into believing that, if they persevere sufficiently, they will
finally discover an esoteric meaning worthy of the mind of the
most enigmatic novelist of the Victorian period. The truth is
that most of what Meredith has to say was anticipated by the
various writers at whom we have been looking. One might say
unkindly that he is occasionally guilty of what probably seemed
to him the ultimate sin, that of *haute vulgarisation*. Rather than
a piece of original speculation, the *Essay* may be seen as the
culmination of the attempt to rid Victorian comic writing of
the incubus of sentimental humour. Our modern unfamiliarity
with Victorian comic theory is more responsible for the
obscurity of the work than is the murky syntax.

What is probably most confusing is that Meredith leaves out
the majority of the critical connectives, expecting his reader to
supply the background against which he is writing. He was
never one to dot his i's, and he preferred here to make glancing
allusions to the problems that had been bothering critics of
comedy. 'This is not meat for little people or for fools,' he
wrote—as epigraph to *Modern Love*, to be sure, but it might
stand for his attitude to the *Essay*. What he is attempting is
what occupied him so often: the meaning of real aristocracy.
The difference, of course, is that here he is talking about an
aristocracy of the intellect, with comedy as the weapon against
the bourgeois values he so despised. As is so frequently apparent
in his other works, the assumption of aristocratic attitudes seems

incompatible to him with straightforward writing that the common man could easily understand.

The circumstances of the writing of the *Essay* are not recorded, but one can imagine that he would have talked about it with his friend and editor, Leslie Stephen, with whose attitudes he was obviously in general sympathy. It is at least possible that part of the obscurity of the work is derivative from their having talked it over so often that Meredith no longer felt much necessity for explanation. Whatever the cause, the reader often has the baffled feeling of reading a private code made up of perfectly ordinary language that simply does not add up to a comprehensible meaning.

The first part of the *Essay* is primarily concerned with drama, but Meredith makes almost no distinction in kind between works for the stage and other comic forms, and he switches easily to fiction without further qualification. The creator of all forms of comedy he calls the comic poet, thus picking up the older, more comprehensive meaning of poet, and at the same time asserting the dignity and validity of comedy in terms that other critics had quarrelled over in arguing whether humour or wit was more closely connected with poetry.

With the same kind of lordly assumption, Meredith bypasses any real definitions of wit and humour. He does, however, make it very clear where his own allegiance lies, by the silent equation of comedy and wit, which two terms he then uses interchangeably. In talking of comedy, he is trying to find a mean between, on the one hand, the agelasts (the non-laughers) and misogelasts (the laughter-haters), and on the other the hypergelasts (the excessive laughers). That mean, for him, is to be found only in the play of wit, which brings 'the slim feasting smile' or, at most, the 'volleys of silvery laughter', in his famous phrase.

Humour, as distinguished from either wit or comedy, Meredith takes to be the province of those who 'have a sentimental objection to face the study of the actual world'. Such sentimentalists feel either disdain or incredulity at reality. 'Humorous writing they will endure, perhaps approve, if it mingles with pathos to shake and elevate the feelings' (p. 13). But this is opposed to common sense, to clear sight, to intelligence: the marks of the Comic Spirit.

H

If you laugh all round [the ridiculous person], tumble him, roll him about, deal him a smack, and drop a tear on him, own his likeness to you, and yours to your neighbour, spare him as little as you shun, pity him as much as you expose, it is a spirit of Humour that is moving you (p. 41).

There are humorists (at least one, anyway: Meredith cites Cervantes) who achieve greatness because of their ability to combine heart and mind in 'an embrace of contrasts beyond the scope of the Comic poet'. Cervantes fuses 'the Tragic sentiment with the Comic narrative', and there are 'lights of Tragedy in his laughter' (pp. 43-4). The compliment to the union of emotion and intellect in the highest forms of humour is a graceful one so far as it goes, but it is not irrelevant that it occupies two brief paragraphs out of more than fifty pages, and one can scarcely avoid the feeling that it is a bit per-functory.

From Cervantes, Meredith moves rapidly downwards to his other major example of humour, Carlyle, who is identified merely as 'a living great, though not creative, humourist'. Carlyle, he tells us, constantly sees the skull beneath the cere-monial robes, the grotesque contrast between man's mortality and his pretension. Yet, for all this, he is insufficiently guided by the cool light of reason. 'This vast power of his, built up of the feelings and the intellect in union, is often wanting in pro-portion and in discretion'. The union is more apparent than real, for such humorists base their choices upon idiosyncrasy rather than intelligent consideration, and 'the feelings are primary, as with singers. Comedy, on the other hand, is an interpretation of the general mind, and is for that reason of necessity kept in restraint' (p. 44).

It is inevitably a distortion of Meredith to quote the relevant sections about humour, for they are inserted so unobtrusively that it is easy to miss seeing how fundamental the attack on sentimental comedy is to the whole *Essay*. To quote them is to give them a prominence he never intended. Tact is not a virtue that one always associates with Meredith, but it is every-where here apparent as he undermines a half-century of comic theory without the over-insistence that would have robbed the argument of its persuasive quality.

Just as Meredith tacitly identifies comedy with wit, so he

assumes, without apparent examination, that comedy is dependent upon incongruity, and that the specific for the resolution of the incongruity is intelligence and common sense. With him it is more than usually appropriate to call the theory of incongruity the intellectual theory. Comedy he says is 'the fountain of sound sense' (p. 14), and it is to be admired, not discounted, for its sparkle. If the comic idea were to prevail with the English, there would be a 'bright and positive, clear Hellenic perception of facts. The vapours of Unreason and Sentimentalism would be blown away before they were productive' (p. 36). There is a predisposition towards comedy in Meredith's countrymen, since they already lean to one aspect of it, that concerned with irony and satire, and they have the prerequisite of comic perception, 'an esteem for common-sense' (p. 39).

They order this matter better in France, however; Molière's plays have no admixture of sentimentality with the wit. Alceste and Tartuffe, Célimène and Philaminte 'are purely comic, addressed to the intellect: there is no humour in them, and they refresh the intellect they quicken to detect their comedy . . .' (p. 42). Too often Meredith's predilection for Molière has been attributed to his liking in his own novels for similitude to stage drama; the fact is that it is less the form he is emulating than the wit, and the chief advantage that the drama offers him is brevity, or spareness, which naturally lends itself to the expression of wit.

One can only wish that Meredith had attempted a fuller definition of wit, for it seems clear that he thought of it as considerably more than the merely verbal, and was only slightly concerned with the element of surprise often attributed to it. In part it would be fair to say that he thought of it in an old-fashioned sense, as the totality of the mental faculties. The comic poet addresses the narrow 'enclosure of men's intellects, with reference to the operation of the social world upon their characters' (p. 45).

In an even more interesting way Meredith seems to have been anticipating twentieth-century views of verbalization, of language as symbol for thought, and to have regarded wit as partaking of the symbolic process. The view is suggested by fragments and hints, rather than put forward in a deliberate

formulation. Constantly comedy and 'the comic idea' are
equated; and over and over he stresses that, as humour deals
with the idiosyncratic and accidental, wit and comedy deal
with philosophic abstractions made concrete by example. 'The
laughter of comedy is impersonal', and it is provoked less by
specific incidents and characters than by the ideas lying behind
them. "It laughs through the mind, for the mind directs it;
and it might be called the humour of the mind" (p. 46).

'Philosopher and Comic poet are of a cousinship in the eye
they cast on life' (p. 15), since they both deal basically with
that which is imperceptible to the senses.

As with the singing of the skylark out of sight, you must love the
bird to be attentive to the song, so in this highest flight of the Comic
Muse, you must love pure Comedy warmly to understand the Misanthrope; you must be receptive of the *idea* of Comedy (p. 23, my
italics).

Menander and Molière are pre-eminent as 'comic poets of the
feelings and the idea. . . . The reason is, that these two poets
idealized upon life: the foundation of their types is real and
in the quick, but they painted with spiritual strength, which
is the solid in Art' (p. 27).

By 'spiritual' and 'idealistic' (which he also frequently
applies to comedy), Meredith did not, of course, mean what
most of his contemporaries would have expected of those terms.
Rather, he is indicating the abstraction present in the 'conception of the Comic that refines even to pain' (p. 27). What is
important about this is that he recognizes in the refining (not
necessarily refined, as we typically use that word) quality of
comedy a kinship to the aspects of wit that are concerned with
definition and distillation of meaning. It is in this sense that
wit need not be confined to the purely verbal, and can certainly transcend it. Hence, he can assert that comedy 'is an
interpretation of the general mind' (p. 44). The same meaning
lies behind his statement that the 'perception of the comic
spirit gives high fellowship' (p. 48). When comedy is removed
from, or is concerned only peripherally with, accidentals, it
becomes a mode of thought and speculation, symbolic in nature,
that is closely allied to poetic creation and perception.

Much of the earlier argument over whether wit or humour

was the higher form of comedy was pretty barren stuff, concerned with theory so dry that it fell into dust at the approach
of reality. Here Meredith is applying himself to the final seriousness of comic art. It would be difficult to overestimate the
importance of this consideration.

What has been taken in Meredith for a boot-licking regard
for the upper classes by some readers is far from that. When the
fully engaged intellect is operating at full stretch, it is idle to
pretend that the process is open to every member of the human
race, let alone little people or fools. A 'simply bourgeois circle'
gives no scope for either comic example or observation. The
middle class needs (as Matthew Arnold knew) 'the brilliant,
flippant, independent upper for a spur and a pattern; otherwise it is likely to be inwardly dull as well as outwardly correct'
(p. 12). Anyone who knows his novels will not need to be told
that he clearly saw the vapidities of the Barbarians; certainly,
he was not postulating any innate superiority of intellect in the
upper classes, only the opportunity there for the cultivation
of honed, refined response. There is an aristocracy of mind
quite as real as that of birth, and it is to that aristocracy that
Meredith addresses his belief in the efficacy of comedy. It is an
attitude that can be understood only when one has firmly in
mind the essentially democratic, even anarchical, anti-intellec-
tual assumptions implicit in the standard nineteenth-century
view of sentimental humour.

Similarly, it becomes easier to understand another puzzling
aspect of the *Essay*, that concerned with the position of women,
when we place it against the background of traditional views
of comedy. It is a critical commonplace that Meredith is one
of the first novelists to depict accurately the nature of the emerg-
ing emancipated woman of the late nineteenth century. The
two major comic characters he treats in the *Essay* are both
women: Millamant in *The Way of the World*, and Célimène in
*Le Misanthrope*, and both are directors of the action because of
their superior wit and intelligence, which elevate them above
the men surrounding them. 'The heroines of Comedy are like
women of the world, not necessarily heartless from being clear-
sighted: they seem so to the sentimentally-reared only for the
reason that they use their wits, and are not wandering vessels
crying for a captain or a pilot' (pp. 14–15).

In the East there is no comedy. 'Where the veil is over
women's faces, you cannot have society, without which the
senses are barbarous and the Comic spirit is driven to the
gutters of grossness to slake its thirst.'

There has been fun in Bagdad. But there never will be civilization
where Comedy is not possible; and that comes of some degree of
social equality of the sexes. . . . But where women are on the road
to an equal footing with men, in attainments and in liberty . . .
there, and only waiting to be transplanted from life to the stage,
or the novel, or the poem, pure Comedy flourishes, and is, as it
would help them to be, the sweetest of diversions, the wisest of
delightful companions (pp. 30–2).

Resounding it is and admirable in its commendation of women,
but one might echo V. S. Pritchett and ask what the devil it
means. The intellect, upon which wit and comedy are based,
is confined to neither man nor woman, and it is not even
primarily sexual in nature. It may be, as Meredith suggests, that
equality of the sexes is a prerequisite for the culture that can
produce comedy. Yet this was certainly not true of the Greek
civilization from which sprang Aristophanes and Menander, to
both of whom Meredith pays tribute. Nor would experience
confirm that only women make good comic characters. Wisely,
Meredith skirts the entire problem of proving that the society
in which Molière (and Célimène) flourished was one in which
there was a demonstrable equality of the sexes.

From the opening page of the *Essay* Meredith is implying the
necessity of the emancipation of women—and the total absence
of it among his contemporaries. 'A society of cultivated men and
women is required, wherein ideas are current and the perceptions quick, that he may be supplied with matter and an audience' (p. 3). In part the work is an attempt to describe an ideal
society in which the healthy scepticism can work beneficently;
the absence of reference to contemporary writers is certainly
his indication of finding the 1870s considerably less than ideal
in this respect. But more than 'matter' would be provided by
such a society. One has the feeling that Meredith is really
appealing for an 'audience', that he is repudiating the common
view that laughter and comedy are inappropriate for well-bred
women. As his regard for aristocracy was not intended to give

greater power to the upper classes, so his statement of the necessity of equality between the sexes is less immediately social than it is a matter of audience. Primarily the *Essay* is concerned with aesthetic matters and with the problems of the comic writer, not social questions, however much the latter may influence the former.

Only when we think of the *Essay* as springing out of a society where 'women are too good to be humorists' can we see how truly Victorian Meredith was, both in his assumption of the beliefs of his contemporaries and in his desire to change them. He could scarcely say, as critic, that his own novels were acceptable to ladies, but he could appeal to the examples of the past to show that women and comedy had always been part of one another. Most important of all, he could try to help establish public thinking that would recognize that narrow boundaries, like those of sex, should not inhibit the appreciation of comedy.

Morality is not a term that Meredith uses lightly, but its application to comedy is everywhere apparent in the *Essay*, as he defends the form against the imputations of grossness. It is not, he says, 'a vile mask'. 'Comedy justly treated, as you find it in Molière, whom we so clownishly mishandled, the Comedy of Molière throws no infamous reflection upon life. It is deeply conceived, in the first place, and therefore it cannot be impure' (pp. 16–17). Much of what passes for morality is mere prejudice passed on from generation to generation. Once it may have had a reason for its disapproval of comedy and the stage, but its survival is due to 'tenacity of national impressions' which 'prod the Puritan nervous system like a satanic instrument; just as one has known Anti-Papists for whom Smithfield was redolent of a sinister smoke . . .' Inherited Puritanism is still met, Meredith says ironically, 'in many families quite undistinguished by arrogant piety' (p. 6).

Finally, Meredith defends comedy against the charge of contemptuous superiority. 'Folly is the natural prey of the Comic', but it cannot be pursued in anger or impatience. 'That is a sign of the absence, or at least of the dormancy, of the Comic idea.' Although comedy pursues folly 'with the springing delight of hawk over heron, hound after fox', it is no longer comedy if it does so with the weapons of satire. 'Contempt is a sentiment that cannot be entertained by comic intelligence' (p. 32).

What Meredith is suggesting here is reminiscent of Leigh Hunt's assertion that in pure mirth 'we triumph, not insolently but congenially; not to anyone's disadvantage, but simply to our own joy and reassurance'.[4] It is superiority without a sting, a theory of incongruity that can make an assessment of value between conflicting attitudes without invoking emotion; 'derisive laughter . . . thwarts the Comic idea. But derision is foiled by the play of the intellect' (p. 46). 'The aim and business of the Comic poet are misunderstood, his meaning is not seized nor his point of view taken, when he is accused of dishonouring our nature and being hostile to sentiment, tending to spitefulness and making an unfair use of laughter' (p. 45)· Comedy is not even dangerous to religion, as the attackers of Shaftesbury had feared, for it is 'only hostile to the priestly element, when that, by baleful swelling, transcends and overlaps the bounds of its office . . .' (p. 48).

The same attitude occurs (in more contorted language) in the 'Prelude' to *The Egoist*: 'In Comedy is the singular scene of charity issuing of disdain under the stroke of honourable laughter: an Ariel released by Prospero's wand from the fetters of the damned witch Sycorax.' The Comic Spirit is never unfriendly 'to the sweetest songfully poetic. Chaucer bubbles with it; Shakespeare overflows . . .' (p. 48). The creatures of great comedy are the creatures of poetry, 'they are of the world enlarged to our embrace by imagination, and by great poetic imagination' (p. 11). This is Meredith's answer to the question of whether comedy and wit proceed from the fancy or the imagination.

Meredith's evocation of the Comic Spirit is probably the best-known description of comedy ever written. Up to this point, in writing about him, I have carefully avoided the passage, since the combination of over-ripe prose and over-familiarity tends towards misunderstanding. If what I have written is clear, the passage should now fall into place as a statement of the general late-Victorian acceptance of the propriety of a comedy that is basically intellectual, witty, incongruous, poetically and symbolically evocative, divorced from contempt, and springing from the totally engaged processes of the mind. The passage was written for persuasion rather than argumentation, and it invites quotation now, not comment:

One excellent test of the civilization of a country, as I have said, I take to be the flourishing of the Comic idea and Comedy; and the test of true Comedy is that it shall awaken thoughtful laughter.

If you believe that our civilization is founded in common-sense (and it is the first condition of sanity to believe it), you will, when contemplating men, discern a Spirit overhead; not more heavenly than the light flashed upward from glassy surfaces, but luminous and watchful; never shooting beyond them nor lagging in the rear; so closely attached to them that it may be taken for a slavish reflex, until its features are studied. It has the sage's brows, and the sunny malice of a faun lurks at the corners of the half-closed lips drawn in an idle wariness of half tension. That slim feasting smile, shaped like the long-bow, was once a big round satyr's laugh, that flung up the brows like a fortress lifted by gunpowder. The laugh will come again, but it will be of the order of the smile, finely tempered, showing sunlight of the mind, mental richness rather than noisy enormity. Its common aspect is one of unsolicitous observation, as if surveying a full field and having leisure to dart on its chosen morsels, without any fluttering eagerness. Men's future upon earth does not attract it; their honesty and shapeliness in the present does; and whenever they wax out of proportion, overblown, affected, pretentious, bombastical, hypocritical, pedantic, fantastically delicate; whenever it sees them self-deceived or hoodwinked, given to run riot in idolatries, drifting into vanities, congregating in absurdities, planning shortsightedly, plotting dementedly; whenever they are at variance with their professions, and violate the unwritten but perceptible laws binding them in consideration one to another; whenever they offend sound reason, fair justice; are false in humility or mined with conceit, individually, or in the bulk—the Spirit overhead will look humanely malign and cast an oblique light on them, followed by volleys of silvery laughter. That is the Comic Spirit (pp. 46–7).

The history might be extended, but it does not seem necessary to press the point. After Meredith there were a few critics who still subscribed to the idea of sentimental humour, but they were in a minority. Oscar Wilde tried desperately to be untypical of his age, but he was never more characteristically late Victorian than when he said that only a man with a heart of stone could fail to laugh at the death of Little Nell. Sentiment has become the butt of comedy not its goal, and the pleasure of the remark is in the playful reversal of ideas to produce an unexpected truth.

It has frequently been said of Meredith, Butler, Wilde, Shaw, and some of the other comic writers of the end of the century that they were 'heartless'. The criticism is not invalid, but it springs from a lingering belief in the amiability of humour, and it neglects the reasons why Victorian comedy had to change its nature or perish. Meredith was probably exaggerating the case when he called comedy 'Light of the mind, the mind's discourse' in his poem 'To the Comic Spirit', but it was an over-emphasis that had to be made if comedy was to pull itself out of the sentiment in which it had been wallowing, and if it was to represent anything like the totality of man's nature.

Short of an intellectual millennium, it is probably too much to expect that most people will ever believe that comedy is serious; human nature is too basically frivolous for that. All the same, the idea is so generally accepted nowadays by thoughtful persons that in a recent novel, *After Julius*, Elizabeth Jane Howard uses the refusal to believe in the seriousness of comedy as a measure of the basically shallow nature of one of her characters:

Esme, as any of her friends would have said, was a practical creature; laughter meant that one was not serious, and apart from Noël Coward and P. G. Wodehouse and stories told by people about friends whom they did not really like, people who seemed to have an aimless desire to find life amusing were simply frivolous—which meant light-hearted in the wrong way. You could be funny about 'characters', and she was definitely not a character. She wanted life to be unreal—and earnest: and with Felix it had been both those things.[5]

That a widely read novelist can make an assumption of like-mindedness on the matter with her readers is sufficient indication of the change that has overtaken comedy since a time when it was universally accepted that it was not a matter worth consideration by responsible men and women.

# NOTES

## Works Frequently Cited

In the last three chapters of this book there are frequent references to the following works. Page and volume citations normally follow quotations within the text. Here, as in the succeeding notes, London is assumed to be the place of publication unless otherwise indicated.

George Combe, *A System of Phrenology*, 2 vols. (Edinburgh, 1843).

George Eliot, 'German Wit: Heinrich Heine', in *Essays*, ed. Thomas Pinney (1968).

Leigh Hunt, *Wit and Humour Selected from the English Poets* (1846); 'On the Combination of Grave and Gay', in *Leigh Hunt's Literary Criticism*, ed. L. H. and C. W. Houtchens (New York, 1956).

George Meredith, 'On the Idea of Comedy and of the Uses of the Comic Spirit', in *Miscellaneous Prose*, Memorial Edition (1910), XXIII.

*Phrenological Journal and Miscellany* (Edinburgh, 1824–37); *Phrenological Journal and Magazine of Moral Science* (1838–47). In theory this was a quarterly, but the title-pages are undated and it appeared so irregularly, that it is often impossible to be certain of the date of individual numbers. When the date is ascertainable, it is given in the text.

Sydney Smith, Lecture X, 'On Wit and Humour'; Lecture XI, 'On Wit and Humour—Part II', in *Elementary Sketches of Moral Philosophy* (1850).

[Leslie Stephen], 'Humour', *Cornhill Magazine*, XXXIII (March 1876), 318–26.

W. M. Thackeray, *The English Humourists; Charity and Humour; The Four Georges*, Everyman (1968).

## Chapter I

[1] 'The Comic Spirit and Victorian Sanity', in *The Reinterpretation of Victorian Literature*, ed. Joseph E. Baker (Princeton, 1950), p. 30.

[2] [Leslie Stephen], 'Humour', *Cornhill Magazine*, XXXIII (March 1876), 318. 'Feminine Humour' (anon.), *Saturday Review*, XXXII (15 July 1871), 75.

[3] 'Hints Towards a Bridgewater Treatise on Laughter' (anon.), *Eclectic Review*, II, n.s. (May 1862), 454–5.

[4] 'Laughter', *Good Words*, X (1 July 1869), 482–3, 486–7. The attitude of general distrust of laughter was not inconsistent with the tone of the magazine.

[5] 'On the Theory of Wit', in *Discourses on Various Subjects* (1852), pp. 244, 242. The essay had been written some years before and first read in public in 1846.

[6] 'Wit and Humour' (anon.), *Westminster Review*, XXIV, n.s. (October 1863), 437. The cause of gravity was consistently upheld in the *Westminster*. Goethe quoted by Harold Nicolson, *The English Sense of Humour and Other Essays* (1956), p. 47.

[7] Quoted by Kathleen Tillotson in *Novels of the Eighteen-Forties* (Oxford, 1965), pp. 56–7.

[8] 'Feminine Humour', *Saturday Review*, XXXII (15 July 1871), 75. 'Philosophy of Laughter' (anon.), *Chambers' Edinburgh Journal*, XVII, n.s. (22 May 1852), 322.

[9] 'Traits of American Humour' (anon.), *Irish Quarterly Review*, II (March 1852), 171.

[10] [J. Fraser?], 'Thomas Hood', *Westminster Review*, XXXIX, n.s. (April 1871), 349.

[11] [Alexander Bain], 'Wit and Humour,' ibid., XLVIII (October 1847), 47, 59; 'Wit and Humour', ibid., XXIV, n.s. (October 1863), 438.

[12] 'Hints Towards a Bridgewater Treatise on Laughter', *Eclectic Review*, II, n.s. (May 1862), 454. [Leslie Stephen], 'American Humour', *Cornhill Magazine*, XIII (January 1866), 41.

[13] In *Characteristics*, ed. J. M. Robertson (1900), I, 10.

[14] Ibid., I, 44.

[15] Ibid., II, 217.

[16] R. L. Brett, *The Third Earl of Shaftesbury: a Study in Eighteenth-Century Literary Theory* (1951), p. 174.

[17] *Characteristics*, I, 85.

[18] A. O. Aldridge, 'Shaftesbury and the Test of Truth', *PMLA*, LX (March 1945), 129.

[19] 'Voltaire', in *Critical and Miscellaneous Essays*, Centenary Edition (1899), I, 412–13.

[20] 'Wit and Humour', *Westminster Review*, XLVIII (October 1847), 55.

[21] 'Hints Towards a Bridgewater Treatise on Laughter', *Eclectic Review*, II, n.s. (May 1862), 459.

[22] *History of English Thought in the Eighteenth Century* (1876), I, 186–7. See also II, 21.

[23] [Sully], 'Ridicule and Truth', *Cornhill Magazine*, XXXV (May 1877), 580–95.

[24] 'Wit and Humour', *Westminster Review*, XXIV, n.s. (October 1863), 436.


*Chapter II*


[1] *Human Nature*, in *English Works of Thomas Hobbes*, ed. Sir William Molesworth (1839, reprinted 1962), IV, 45–6, 56.

[2] Sully, *An Essay on Laughter* (1902), pp. 125–6.

[3] *Kant's Kritik of Judgment*, tr. J. H. Bernard (1892), pp. 223–5.

[4] *The World as Will and Representation*, ed. E. F. J. Payne (Indian Hills, Colorado, 1958), I, 59; II, 91.

[5] *The Table Talk and Omniana*, ed. T. Ashe (1884), p. 256; 'Wit and

Humour', in *Coleridge's Miscellaneous Criticism*, ed. T. M. Raysor (1936), pp. 445, 440.

6 *Wit and Humour Selected from the English Poets* (1846), pp. 9, 7.

7 [R. A. Wilmott], 'Wit and Humour', *Fraser's Magazine*, XXXIV (December 1846), 742.

8 'Wit and Humour', *Westminster Review*, XLVIII (October 1847), 34.

9 'Philosophy of Laughter' (anon.), *Chambers' Edinburgh Journal*, XVII (22 May 1852), 322.

10 'The Evolution of Humour', *National Review*, X (February 1888), 813–14. See also E. S. Dallas, *The Gay Science* (1866), II, 54–7. The view has held on, improbably, into the twentieth century; see DeWitt H. Parker, *The Principles of Aesthetics* (New York, 1947), p. 94.

11 *Miscellaneous Criticism*, p. 442.

12 *The Life of John Sterling*, Centenary Edition (1897), p. 57.


*Chapter III*

1 Stuart Tave, *The Amiable Humorist* (Chicago, 1960), viii. The last sentence seems to me a slight overstatement, as I hope the present book makes clear.

2 From *Critical and Miscellaneous Essays*: 'Jean Paul Friedrich Richter', II, 143; 'Jean Paul Friedrich Richter', I, 14–17; 'Schiller', II, 200.

3 Oxford Illustrated Dickens (1947), xii.

4 'John Paul Frederick Richter', in *Collected Writings*, ed. David Masson (Edinburgh, 1890), XI, 263, 270.

5 *Wit and Humour Selected from the English Poets* (1846), p. 11.

6 'Wit and Humour', *Hogg's Instructor*, V, n.s. (1850), 167, 181. The choice of Thersites as an example of a witty character indicates Whipple's ideas about wit.

7 [Collins], 'American Humour', *British Quarterly Review*, LII (October 1870), 324, 325, 350.

8 [Massey], 'American Humour', *North British Review*, XXXIII (November 1860), 462, 472, 461.

9 'Doctor Pentagram' [T. C. Irwin], 'Wit', *Dublin University Magazine*, LXII (July 1863), 38; [Massey], 'American Humour', *North British Review*, XXXIII (November 1860), 463; [Collins], 'American Humour', *British Quarterly Review*, LII (October 1870), 324; 'Feminine Humour', *Saturday Review*, XXXII (15 July 1871), 75; J. H. Shorthouse, 'The Humorous in Literature', in *Literary Remains*, ed. by his wife (1905), II, 261, 273; William Minto, *A Manual of English Prose Literature* (1872), p. 27.

10 'Wit and Humour', *Hogg's Instructor*, V, n.s. (1850), 167.

11 *Leviathan, English Works*, III, 56–8. *Human Nature*, IV, 45–6; IV, 56.

12 *Essay Concerning Human Understanding*, ed. A. C. Fraser (Oxford, 1894), I, 203–4.

13 'H' [Horace Smith], 'The Wisdom of Laughter', *New Monthly Magazine*, V (1822), 459.

14 'H. W.', 'Yankeeana', *London and Westminster Review*, XXXII (December 1838), 138–9.

15 Frances Power Cobbe, 'The Humour of Various Nations', *Victoria Magazine*, I (July 1863), 194.

16 'Wit and Humour' (anon.), *British Quarterly Review*, LVI (July 1872), 45. During the 1850s and 1860s there was a constant stream of considerations of the nature of national humour, particularly American. A few examples are: 'Traits of American Humour', *Irish Quarterly Review*, II (March 1852), 171; [George Eliot], 'German Wit: Heinrich Heine', *Westminster Review*, LXV (January 1856), 1; [Gerald Massey], 'American Humour', *North British Review*, XXXIII, (November 1860), 461; 'American Humour' (anon.), *All the Year Around*, VI (16 November 1861), 190; [James Crawford], 'Scottish Humour', *North British Review*, XXXV (November 1861), 480; [T. C. Irwin], 'Wit', *Dublin University Magazine*, LXII (July 1863), 38; [Leslie Stephen], 'American Humour', *Cornhill Magazine*, XIII (January 1866), 28; [James Hannay], 'Recent Humourists: Aytoun, Peacock, Prout', *North British Review*, VI, n.s. (September 1866), 75; [Gerald Massey], 'Yankee Humour', *Quarterly Review*, CXXII (January 1867), 212; [Mortimer Collins], 'American Humour', *British Quarterly Review*, LII (October 1870), 324.

17 'American Humour', *North British Review*, XXXIII (November 1860), 462–3.

18 [Bain], 'Wit and Humour', *Westminster Review*, XLVIII (October 1847), 47–8; Hunt, *Wit and Humour Selected from the English Poets* (1846), p. 14; [Morley], 'Byron', *Fortnightly Review*, VIII, n.s. (1 December 1870), 655; Pater, 'Charles Lamb', in *Appreciations* (1910), p. 105.

19 [Massey], 'American Humour', *North British Review*, XXXIII (November 1860), 463; [Irwin], 'Wit', *Dublin University Magazine*, LXII (July 1863), 38; Coleridge, *Shakespearean Criticism*, ed. T. M. Raysor (1930), II, 124.

20 D. J. Gray, 'Humor as Poetry in Nineteenth-Century English Criticism', *Journal of English and Germanic Philology*, LXI (1962), 25. This is, so far as I can determine, the only study of this aspect of comic theory.

21 Carlyle, 'Voltaire', *Critical and Miscellaneous Essays*, I, 451; George Eliot, 'German Wit: Heinrich Heine', *Essays*, ed. Thomas Pinney (1968), pp. 218–19.

22 'English Comedy' (anon.), *Broadway Magazine*, II, n.s. (July 1869), 383.

23 pp. 18, 200–3. The complaints were widespread; see, for example, 'The Principles of Comedy' (anon.), *Tinsley's Magazine*, VI (February 1870), 86; 'English Comedy' (anon.), *Dublin University Magazine*, LXXXII (December 1873), 747; 'F' [Percy Fitzgerald?], 'Modern Comedy', *Fraser's Magazine*, IX, n.s. (February 1874), 235.

24 [Edmund Yates?], 'Comic Literature', *Temple Bar*, IX (1863), 590–1.

25 H. A. Taine, *History of English Literature*, tr. H. van Laun (Edinburgh, 1874), IV, 291, 140, 175, 202, 176, 165, 137–8, 173, 176–7.

26 Penthorne, 'Vis Comica', *Belgravia*, XXIV (September 1874), 331; 'Victoria Discussion Society' (anon.), *Victoria Magazine*, XXIII (June 1874), 123.

27 'Wit and Humour', *Westminster Review*, XXIV, n.s. (October 1863), 467.

28 [Collins], 'American Humour', *British Quarterly Review*, LII (October 1870), 350, 326, 351.

29 'Wit and Humour', *British Quarterly Review*, LVI (July 1872), 43–9.

30 'On the Comic Writers of England', *Gentleman's Magazine*, VI, n.s. (April 1871), 507–9.

31 'Wit', *Irish Monthly*, V (1877), 343, 341, 414, 578.

*Chapter IV*

1 'Jean Paul Friedrich Richter', *Critical and Miscellaneous Essays*, II, 96.

2 *Statistics of Phrenology* (1836), p. 2.

3 Watson, p 3.

4 John D. Davies, *Phrenology: Fad and Science* (New Haven, 1955), p. 10.

5 p. 11.

6 William Scott, 'Of Wit and the Feeling of the Ludicrous', *Phrenological Journal*, IV (1827), 195–6.

7 'On the Functions of Combativeness, Destructiveness, and Secretiveness', *Transactions of the Phrenological Society* (Edinburgh, 1827), pp. 173–4.

8 2 vols. (Edinburgh, 1843).

9 'John Paul Frederick Richter', *Collected Writings*, XI, 270.

*Chapter V*

1 [R. A. Wilmott], 'Wit and Humour', *Fraser's Magazine*, XXXIV (December 1846), 736; 'Leigh Hunt's Wit and Humour', by 'A', *Dublin University Magazine*, XXIX (January 1847), 80.

2 Quoted by Gordon N. Ray, *Thackeray: the Age of Wisdom* (1958), p. 143.

3 E.g. ibid., p. 142.

4 Ibid., p. 214.

*Chapter VI*

1 For example, this essay itself is usually credited with being the most influential introduction of Heine to the English reading public.

2 The original title was 'On the Idea of Comedy and the Uses of the Comic Spirit', and among the other titles under which it has been published is *An Essay on Comedy and the Uses of the Comic Spirit*.

3 *George Meredith and English Comedy* (1970), p. 25.

4 *Wit and Humour Selected from the English Poets* (1846), p. 7.

5 Elizabeth Jane Howard, *After Julius* (Jonathan Cape, London, 1965), p. 79. Quoted with permission of the publisher.